THE ROBIN HOOD WALKS

DEDICATION

To the memory of the late Councillor Malcolm Lee, who,
in his capacity as Chairman of the Environmental
Committee of Nottinghamshire County Council,
gave his wholehearted support to our venture.

THE ROBIN HOOD WALKS

A comprehensive Guide to walks in Robin Hood country including the Third Edition of the Guide to the full route of Nottinghamshire's first Recreational Footpath, THE ROBIN HOOD WAY.

The Robin Hood Way
was planned by members of the
Nottingham Wayfarers' Rambling Club
in commemoration of its
Golden Jubilee year in 1982
from an idea by Christopher Thompson.

Maps by Michael Mitchell and Jeff Nightingale.
Sketches by Michael Mitchell and Neil Alderson.

CORDEE LEICESTER

ISBN 1 871890 02 0

British Library Cataloguing in Publication Data
A catalogue record for this book is available from the British Library

We hope this Guide will enable and encourage people to enjoy walking some of the footpaths in Nottinghamshire, especially The Robin Hood Way and the circular walks radiating from it, and thus to help to preserve these paths for future generations.
Although every effort has been made to keep the Guide as clear and accurate as possible, we are sorry that we cannot take any responsibility for your walks or wanderings, so please take care.

All trade enquiries to:
Cordee, 3a De Montfort Street, Leicester LE1 7HD

This book is available from specialist equipment shops and booksellers in the area. It can, along with all the maps mentioned in the text be obtained direct from the publishers. Please write for a copy of our comprehensive stocklist of outdoor recreation and travel books/maps.

Cover photographs by Gordon Gadsby, Beeston

Printed and bound in Great Britain by
The Guernsey Press Co. Ltd, Guernsey, Channel Islands

ACCESS POINTS TO THE ROBIN HOOD WAY

1. Nottingham Castle
2. University Park (Highfields entrance)
3. Wollaton Park
4. Bramcote Park
5. Strelley village
6. Kimberley
7. Greasley church
8. Bulwell Hall Park
9. Bestwood Country Park
10. Burntstump Park
11. Blidworth Forest sites
12. Blidworth village
13. Newstead Abbey
14. Thieves Wood Car Park
15. Baulker Lane Forest Site (Blidworth)
16. Farnsfield
17. Southwell
18. Kirklington station
19. Eakring village
20. Rufford Abbey Country Park
21. Archway House (lay-by on A.6075)
22. Fanny's Grove Car Park
23. Creswell Crags Visitor Centre
24. Clumber Park (Main Car Park or Hardwick Grange)
25. Crookford
26. Haughton (B.6387)
27. Whitewater Bridge
28. Sherwood Forest Visitor Centre

N.B. Please park in proper access points. **DO NOT** cause any obstruction to farmers and local people by improper parking.

ACKNOWLEDGEMENTS

Our thanks go to all the people and organisations listed below for their support, advice and encouragement at every stage of planning, without which the project would not have been completed nor the Guide produced.

Countryside Commission. National Trust. Forestry Commission. Welbeck Estates. British Waterways Board. British Coal. Various District Councils. University of Nottingham. Local History Library. City Information Bureau.
Nottinghamshire County Council: (a) Footpaths Officers; (b) Planning & Economic Development; (c) Visitor Centres Ranger Service & Spadework. Neil Alderson.
Michael Mitchell for route maps of the Robin Hood Way.
Jeff Nightingale for maps of the circular walks.
Malcolm McKenzie (Newark Area, Ramblers' Association) and Nottinghamshire County Council for circular walks. Eric Horriben for historical information.
Nottingham Wayfarers' Rambling Club for initial support and Club members for their assistance with the original planning.
Last but not least the Committee members who put so much time and effort into negotiating and setting up the route and the current revisions: Chris Thompson, Roland Price, Alec and Lesley Hickton, Joan Barks, John Cooke, Janet & Geoff Rix; and Sue Andrews for help with the typing. Also anyone whose name we have omitted.

CONTENTS

FOREWORD

The idea of the Robin Hood Way was first put forward in 1980 by Chris Thompson, then Social Secretary of the Nottingham Wayfarers' Rambling Club. It soon had the Club's support, and from early 1981 work was in the hands of a Sub-Committee of three: Chris, Alec Hickton and myself. This led to the official opening of the Way in May 1985 and the original Guide.

There are approximately 2000 miles of registered footpaths and bridle-ways in Nottinghamshire, which is about the same as the total length of all the roads in the County, and we felt that it was time that an attempt was made to link some of them into a continuous route with a theme, as had been done in many other Counties. Thus we hoped to remove the dubious distinction that Nottinghamshire had, of being the only East Midlands County without a properly designated and named Recreational Footpath.

The most appropriate theme seemed obviously to be our most famous character, the outlaw Robin Hood, who has connections with many places in both City and County. Whether he was legend or living person is not our concern – his exploits have captured the imagination of many thousands of people over the years, and are of continuing interest. The fact that Robin Hood Country is so often sought out by the tourist convinced us that the theme was worth developing.

But the places with connections with Robin Hood are well scattered around the County, so how could they be linked? There exist, through the efforts of various Councils, several Country Parks and other public open spaces throughout the County; there are also other sites which we felt to be worthy of inclusion in our route and which, not entirely by accident, gave us better options for walking from one point to another. Thus the Way links not only those places which fit our theme, but also many others which are of interest for one or more of several other reasons.

Many of these other sites also form alternative Access Points to the Way, enabling walkers to join the route at different places to suit themselves, and to walk the route in short sections if they wish. At the same time many of these Access Points form links with circular walks that can be undertaken either in conjunction with sections of the Way or as separate walks, and we have included 14 of these circular walks in the new Guide.

The existence of so many miles of footpaths and bridleways has enabled us to ensure that over 90% of the route is on existing rights-of-way or County roads. Where this is not the case, the Way crosses public open spaces, or in a few instances is on 'permissive paths', which are so described in the Guide. We hope to take notice of future developments in the provision of public amenities and to incorporate them into the route when possible and beneficial, so that the route will be under constant revision.

We cannot, unfortunately, claim that there is a tremendous variety of scenery in Nottinghamshire north of the Trent, but we have tried to include a good mixture of what there is, combining urban walking, parkland, waterside paths, agricultural land and woodland, plus our only real outcrop of limestone. There are no really big hills, but a good deal of the route is over pleasantly undulating countryside.

The Robin Hood Way was Nottingham Wayfarers' Rambling Club's willing contribution to the public's enjoyment of the County's rights-of-way, in celebration of the Club's Golden Jubilee in 1982. Elsewhere we acknowledge our debt to the many people whose help made it possible, but we must not forget also the Club members who originally helped to verify the route by walking it, and not least our wives and families, who put up with our frequent absences whilst working on the project.

We hope that we have mentioned everyone whose support and co-operation were so valuable; if not, we apologise. Our special thanks are due to the different Departments of Nottinghamshire County Council, and most of all to Gordon Jones, Senior Footpaths Officer, and his colleagues – without the enormous amount of work they, too, put into the scheme, especially in the area of path maintenance and waymarking, the Robin Hood Way would never have come to fulfilment.

ROLAND PRICE
(Former Chairman)
Nottingham Wayfarers' Rambling Club.

PREFACE

The first two Editions of the Robin Hood Way Guide sold almost 5000 copies in less than eight years, so a third one became necessary. Minor changes in the route due to altered field boundaries, footpath diversions, and both rural and urban developments, have added to this need. In addition to these enforced changes, we have taken the opportunity of including what we hope will prove to be improvements to the Way. Some of these are adjustments to the route to include short stretches where we were not entirely happy about the original chosen line (as at Kimberley and Watnall).

There are also some major changes to the route, the largest of which is the inclusion of Southwell in Sections 9 and 10. We always felt unhappy that we had not included a visit to this tiny Cathedral City, but at the time we felt that it was perhaps rather too far off the direct route. On reflection, however, we now believe that we can no longer deprive walkers of the chance to visit that gem of Norman architecture which is Southwell Minster, especially as we have been able to add to the route some very pleasant walking country, including another Robin Hood Hill. Also it so happens that Southwell now falls just about halfway along the route – a good excuse for a day off! Further, in improving the route around Kimberley, so as to reduce the amount of walking in built-up areas, we have been able to bring in some attractive countryside around Greasley and to include the option of a short detour to the site of Greasley Castle.

The changes to the actual route now brings the length of the Robin Hood Way to over 100 miles, another notable landmark in its development.

Since the first Guide was published, there have been many changes in the public transport network, mainly due to the de-regulation of bus services. We have decided, therefore, to delete all transport information previously given, especially as up-to-date information can be obtained from the 'Bus Hotline', Telephone Nottingham 240000.

A lot of the 'useful' information included in the previous Editions has also been deleted, as it became impossible to keep up with changes. Any information which readers may need and which is not included here may easily be obtained from the various Tourist Information Bureaux throughout the County.

The other major change to this book is that we have now included the descriptions of 14 Circular Walks based on Sections of the Robin Hood Way. Though some of these appear in other publications, such as the Nottinghamshire County Council's series of Walks Leaflets (obtainable from Trent Bridge House) and Malcolm McKenzie's collections of Nottinghamshire walks, and have been adapted from these, it was thought that many walkers, especially families, would be more interested in short circular walks than a long linear route, and that other walkers, having tackled the whole route, might want to revisit some of their favourite areas, so that it would be preferable to cater for these walkers in the same volume; a view which was acceded to by contacts in the book trade.

Since the Robin Hood Way was opened, we have formed the Robin Hood Way Association, which is open to anyone who has either walked the Way, plans to do so, or who is sympathetic to our desire to ensure the continued success of the Way. Membership is secured by a once-for-all payment, and the subscription includes a free cloth badge. A Certificate is available on payment of a small charge, to anyone who can show that they have travelled the whole route, and the cloth badge is also available for sale.

For further information about the Robin Hood Way Association, please contact either:

Roland Price	or	Chris Thompson
23 The Hollows		21 Spindle View
Wilford		Calverton
Nottingham		Nottingham
NG11 7FJ		NG14 6HF
Tel: 817976		Tel: 653318

ROUTE FINDING WITH THE GUIDE

The route of the Robin Hood Way has been divided into 18 Sections of varying length, each of them walkable within a day, though Section 9 could conveniently be divided into two. Each Section has Access Points either at, or close to, both start and finish. As most tourists looking for Robin Hood start in Nottingham, the route is described from Nottingham Castle, i.e. from south to north, though in general the waymarking indicates both directions.

The description of each Section is complemented by sketch maps, the numbers on the maps corresponding to the paragraphs in the description. We believe that the symbols used on the maps will be clear to walkers, who should be familiar with maps. Whilst we also believe, after repeated checking, that it should be possible to follow the route with the sketch maps, descriptions and waymarks alone, we advise walkers also to carry the 1:50,000 Ordnance Survey Landranger Maps, Sheets 129 (Nottingham and Loughborough) and 120 (Mansfield, Worksop and surrounding area) to help confirm the route and also assist with the identification of road numbers and in general orientation. The larger scale 1:25,000 Pathfinder Maps would also be useful in locating such details as field boundaries, but are not essential, especially as boundaries frequently change.

The route description includes precise details of starting points for each Section, and at the end of each Section some brief notes are given on the various places and features seen on the Way. These have been kept separate from the route descriptions, as it is anticipated that readers will wish to study the notes before setting out on the day's walk. For further study, reference may be made to the County Library and to any good bookshop.

We hope you will enjoy walking at least partly in the footsteps of the Outlaw of Sherwood Forest. Please remember that the countryside is someone's workshop and livelihood, and that most of the Way runs through land devoted to farming and forestry. Please respect the countryman's handiwork, keep precisely on the described route, and always observe the Countryside Code.

As Robin Hood himself might have said to anyone seeking to track him down in the places he visited – GOOD HUNTING AND THE BEST OF LUCK!

THE COUNTRYSIDE CODE

Guard against all risk of fire.
Plantations, woodland and heaths are highly inflammable: every year acres burn because of casually dropped matches, cigarette ends or pipe ash.

Fasten all gates.
Even if you find gates open, fasten them behind you. Animals cannot be told to stay where they're put. A gate left open invites them to wander, a danger to themselves, to crops and to traffic.

Keep dogs under proper control.
Farmers have good reason to regard visiting dogs as pests; in the country a

civilised town dog can become a savage. Keep your dog on lead wherever there is livestock about, also on country roads.

Keep to the paths across farm land.
Crops can be ruined by people's feet. Remember that grass is a valuable crop too, sometimes the only one on the farm. Flattened corn or hay is very difficult to harvest. Keep to the waymarked route and maintain single file when walking across land with crops.

Avoid damaging fences, hedges and walls.
They are expensive items in the farm's economy; repairs are costly and use scarce labour. Keep to recognised routes, using gates and stiles.

Leave no litter.
All litter is unsightly and some is dangerous as well. Take litter home for disposal; in the country it costs a lot to collect it.

Safeguard water supplies.
Your chosen walk may well cross a catchment area for the water supply of millions. Avoid polluting it in any way. Never interfere with cattle troughs.

Protect wild life, wild plants and trees.
Wild life is best observed, not collected. To pick or uproot flowers, carve trees and rocks, or destroy wild animals and birds, destroys other people's pleasure as well.

Go carefully on country roads.
Country roads have special dangers; blind corners, high banks and hedges, slow-moving tractors and farm machinery or animals. Motorists should reduce their speed and take extra care; walkers should keep to the right, facing oncoming traffic.

Respect the life of the countryside.
Set a good example and try to fit in with the life and work of the countryside. This way good relations are preserved, and those who follow are not regarded as enemies.

OBSTRUCTIONS

If you find your right-of-way obstructed (by barbed wire, by aggressive bulls in fields, by misleading notices, by landowners or their agents, by locked gates or broken bridges or stiles), please report details to the Senior Footpaths Officer, Planning & Economic Development, Nottinghamshire County Council, Trent Bridge House, West Bridgford, Nottingham, NG2 6BJ (Tel: Nottingham (774483), who will take the necessary action.

1. NOTTINGHAM CASTLE TO WOLLATON PARK

Distance: 6.5 km. (4 miles)

Maps: Landranger Sheet 129.   1:25,000 Series Sheet SK.53.

Start: Nottingham Castle Gateway.

How to get there: From the Old Market Square, walk away from the Council House front, across the paved square to the left-hand corner (public toilets), then straight up the road opposite (Friar Lane). Use the subway under Maid Marian Way and continue up Friar Lane to the Castle Gateway.

There are frequent buses from all parts of the City to the Old Market Square, Maid Marian Way, Friar Lane or Trinity Square. From the Bus Stations at Broad Marsh and Victoria Centres, and from the Midland Railway Station, follow the signs for the Old Market Square or the Castle. Guides and Street Maps of Nottingham can be obtained from most bookshops, or from the Information Centre, Smithy Row (which is situated underneath the Council House building).

THE ROUTE

N.B. UNIVERSITY PARK AND WOLLATON PARK ARE CLOSED AT DUSK. THEREFORE SECTION 1 AND THE FIRST PART OF SECTION 2 CAN ONLY BE WALKED DURING DAYLIGHT HOURS.

1. Starting from the Robin Hood Way plaque, on the wall outside the Castle

Gateway (A), go to the junction of Friar Lane and Castle Road, turn sharp right, pass Castle Lawn (B) and continue down the hill parallel to the Castle walls (C).

2. Turn right into the forecourt of the 'Trip to Jerusalem' Inn (D), then pass through the iron gates into Brewhouse Yard (EA). Should these gates be locked, continue down to the road junction, turn right and go to the pelican crossing as in point 3 below.

3. Leave Brewhouse Yard by the lower gate, on to a wide road, Castle Boulevard (F) and cross by a pelican crossing. Turn left on the other side and walk to the road junction with traffic lights.

4. Turn right on to Wilford Street and walk to the bridge over the Canal (G). On the far side of the bridge the Canal Towpath (H) is signposted.

5. Turn right, go down the steps to the canal side near a lock gate and follow the towpath for about 2 km. (1¼ miles). (On the way you will pass a Marina, a railway bridge and a road bridge by a boat-building yard.) The canal then bears left, and the next bridge over it carries the Ring Road A.614.

6. Take the flight of steps leading up on to this bridge and turn right, going downhill towards a large traffic island. At the bottom, take a path to the right leading to a subway under the road. Having passed under the road, turn right again and reach the traffic island.

7. Turn left and walk along Beeston Road, crossing it at a pedestrian crossing. Walk to University Park, ignore the main vehicle entrance, but take the first pedestrian entrance some 200 metres further.
NOTE: The path through University Park is closed at dusk. It will also *not* be waymarked.

8. Go through the gate, follow path towards Lakeside Pavilion, then turn left and walk alongside the Lake into University Park (J), following the main path and ignoring all deviations. At the far end of the Lake, near the site of an old paddling pool, bear left to reach University Boulevard just before a traffic island.

9. Turn right, walk to a second island, then turn right into the University Campus (K) through the West Entrance and continue along Beeston Lane. After approx. 1 km. (0.6 miles), shortly after passing the entrance to the University Sports and Social Club on the left, take a passage between houses (known locally as a 'twitchell') on the left, to reach Derby Road.

0. Cross Derby Road (A.52) at the pelican crossing just to the right, then go through a gate between the two sides of a building, Beeston Lodge, just to the left, and enter Wollaton Park.

1. Walk straight on into the Park until reaching the Lake side. Turn right and take the tree-lined path to Wollaton Hall.

N.B. THE ROUTE THROUGH THE UNIVERSITY CAMPUS IS NOT AT PRESENT A RIGHT-OF-WAY, AND MAY BE CLOSED AT ANY TIME. BY AGREEMENT WITH THE UNIVERSITY, IT IS NOT WAYMARKED.
 IF THIS PATH IS CLOSED, THE ROUTE FROM POINT 7 TO THE END OF SECTION 1 IS AS FOLLOWS:

a. At the island, take the crossing straight ahead.

b. After crossing the road, follow the pavement rising slightly past the University Hospital to the right, to another large traffic island with a vehicle underpass.

c. Cross the Derby Road A.52 at the pelican crossing and continue straight ahead along Middleton Boulevard for 200 metres until you reach the gates at the entrance to Wollaton Park, set back to your left.

d. Turn left through the gates and follow the tree-lined avenue (Lime Tree Avenue), passing through a handgate where the road to the Golf Course leads off to the left. Continue down Lime Tree Avenue as far as Wollaton Hall. **NOTE: Wollaton Park is closed at dusk.**

REFRESHMENTS

'Trip to Jerusalem' Inn   Historical Inn built into the Castle Rock (See Notes.) Traditional ales.

'Salutation' Inn   Historical Inn with cave cellars. Bar meals. Traditional ales.

INTEREST

Old Market Square and other places of interest in the City are described in various published Guides.

A. NOTTINGHAM CASTLE   This is not the mediaeval Castle, but the former palace of the Duke of Newcastle, built 1679, seriously damaged by the Reform Bill Rioters in 1831, and restored in 1875–8 as a Museum. Among the Museum' features are the Gibbs collection of English silver, a collection of paintings b local artists of national repute, and mediaeval Nottingham alabaster carvings Recent excavations have brought to light some parts of the original Castle, which are now open to the public. One of the main attractions is the guided tour of the series of caves in the sandstone rock on which the Castle stands. (Details from the Castle.) The Castle Gateway, restored mediaeval, incorporates a shop devoted to the sale of Robin Hood and other souvenirs, and a special display about Robin Hood and his Merry Men. The Castle Green, inside the grounds and near the Gateway, stands above the Inner Bailey of the original Castle. The outline of the Royal Castle has been marked out following excavations. For opening hours of the Castle and grounds, see the Notice board just inside the Gateway, or enquire from the Information Bureau. Admission is free except at weekends and Bank Holidays.

B. CASTLE LAWN   This open area, part grass, part paved, stands in the dry outer moat of the Castle, on the site of the former Riding School, with the mediaeval walls visible. The large arch over the moat replaced the drawbridge On the lawn stands a controversial statue of Robin Hood by James Woodford, a local sculptor, which was placed here in 1952, with plaques depicting other members of Robin's 'band'. Across the road stands 'Severn's Building', a mediaeval house dating from 1450, which originally stood in Middle Pavement. It was moved to this site 'en bloc' when the Broad Marsh Centre was built in 1969, and has been converted into the Lace Centre, devoted to the history and sale of the world-famous Nottingham Lace. Hand-made lace is still made at the Centre.

C. CASTLE WALLS   Note the numerous entrances into the Castle rock below the walls, now mainly used as storerooms.

D. 'TRIP TO JERUSALEM' INN   Dating from A.D. 1189, it claims to be the oldest Inn in England. Some of the rooms are built into the Castle rock and at certain times the landlord will take small parties around the cellars, used at various periods of history as dungeons and as a brewhouse, or round other rock-cut rooms. (Open during normal licensing hours.)

E. BREWHOUSE YARD   Formerly a 2-acre parish outside the jurisdiction of the old town, this yard originally contained a brew house and a mill. Nearly all the houses in the yard had at one time or another served as taverns during the 18th and 19th centuries, and the area did develop a bad reputation. Five of these brick-built Town Houses, built around 1670, have been imaginatively converted into a Museum of Daily Life. In addition to the regular displays, where one can step back in time to an old school, shops and domestic rooms, special exhibitions are arranged from time to time. (Open daily except Christmas Day, admission free.) In the garden in the Spring will be found some examples of the Nottingham Crocus, now rare, but which once grew in profusion in the fields between the old town and the River Trent, until they were built on during the expansion of the City in the late 19th century, to become the residential area still called 'The Meadows'.

F. CASTLE BOULEVARD   One of several fine 'boulevards' forming the Inner Ring Road of Nottingham, this road runs over part of the former course of the River Leen, which was diverted at the time of the boulevard's construction, to flow into the Nottingham and Beeston Canal. That particular stretch of the Leen was itself a diversion made by the Normans.

G. NOTTINGHAM AND BEESTON CANAL   The canal is 6 miles (9½ km.) long and runs from the Trent at Meadow Lane Lock near Trent Bridge, back to the Trent at Beeston Lock. It is part of a system made to render the Trent navigable from the Humber to Shardlow in Derbyshire, was opened in 1796, and was built to carry coal into the City.

H. CANAL TOWPATH WALK   The Canal has been landscaped and opened as a Trail from its junction with the Trent near Trent Bridge. Details of this walk and of narrow-boat trips can be obtained from the Canal Museum, a museum of canal life converted from a canal warehouse. This Museum is situated a short way back along the canal from where the Robin Hood Way joins it at Wilford Street bridge. It is on the city side of the canal, and is reached by walking to the left along the canal as far as the next road bridge, up on to the road, Carrington Street, just below the Midland Station, turning left to a road junction, then left again for some 50 metres. The entrance is in a yard at the side of an Inn with its own brewhouse.

J. UNIVERSITY PARK   A City Park in the grounds of the University of Nottingham, with an attractive tree-fringed Lake which is frequented by waterfowl, and on which boats can be hired in the summer. The route along the lower side of the Lake is extremely beautiful in Spring, being bordered by many azalea and rhododendron bushes of various colours, and is well provided with seats. There are good views of the University buildings. **University Park is closed at dusk.** Refreshments can be obtained from the University Arts Centre during most daylight hours, except on Sundays. The Arts Centre is situated close to the main vehicle entrance to the University.

K. UNIVERSITY OF NOTTINGHAM Developed from the Adult School of 1798 and University College in Shakespeare Street in the City (now part of the Nottingham Trent University), the present University was built on land presented by Sir Jesse Boot, the founder of Boots the Chemists, who later became Lord Trent. It was opened by King George V in 1928 and has expanded greatly in recent years, so there are many new buildings on the Campus, whilst its reputation as a seat of learning has also grown. The bust of Lord Trent can be seen at an entrance to the Park further along University Boulevard, opposite the clock tower of the University.

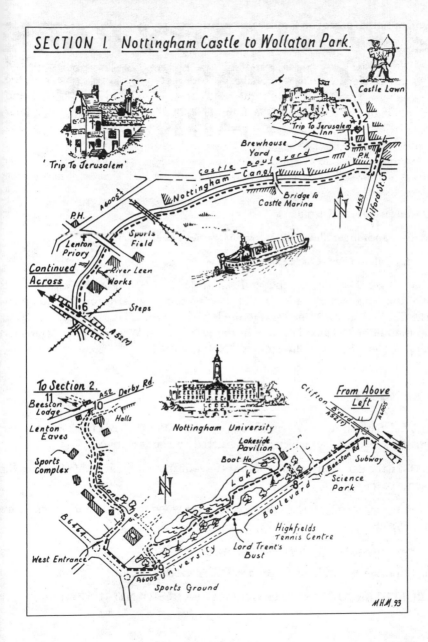

SECTION 1. Nottingham Castle to Wollaton Park.

'Trip To Jerusalem'

Castle Lawn

Trip To Jerusalem Inn

Brewhouse Yard
Boulevard
P.H.

Castle Canal
Nottingham

Bridge to
Castle Marina

P.H.

Lenton Priory

Sports Field

River Leen Works

Continued Across

Steps

A52(T)

To Section 2.

A52 Derby Rd.

Beeston Lodge

Halls

Lenton Eaves

Sports Complex

B6464

West Entrance

A6005

Nottingham University

From Above Left

Clifton Bridge A52(T)

Lakeside Pavilion

Boat Ho.

Lake

Boulevard

Beeston Rd

Subway

Science Park

Highfields Tennis Centre

Lord Trent's Bust

University

Sports Ground

M.H.M. 93

2. WOLLATON PARK TO BRAMCOTE PARK

Distance: 4.5 km. (2.8 miles.)

Maps: Landranger Sheet 129.   1:25,000 Series Sheet SK.53.

Start: Wollaton Park Car Park.

How to get there: By car, follow Ilkeston Road (A.609) from the City towards Wollaton village, forking left at traffic lights to follow signs for Wollaton Park. The Car Park is inside the Park, to the left off the road. From the Car Park walk up the hill to Wollaton Hall to join the Robin Hood Way. For public transport services, telephone the 'Bus Hotline' (Nottm. 240000).

THE ROUTE

1. Walk to the front of Wollaton Hall (A), and with the Hall behind you descend the steps to the stables which can be entered by a large archway.

2. Take the path going downhill past the refreshment room and follow it to the corner of the Lake.

3. Bear slightly right on to a shale path with a wood to the left, and go through a bridlegate.

4. Pass through a wooden gate, then a gate in a wall.

5. Continue ahead along a short drive to a road (Parkside).

FROM HERE TO POINT 12 IS THROUGH A RESIDENTIAL AREA.

Cross Parkside and descend the short street opposite (Wollaton Rise) to its junction with a major road (Wollaton Vale).

Go left along Wollaton Vale for a few metres, then cross it to enter Woodbank Drive.

Go along Woodbank Drive for about 100 metres.

Turn first left into Vines Cross and continue to its junction with Appledore Avenue.

0. Turn left along Appledore Avenue, following it as it curves right.

1. At the end of the curve, turn right into a cul-de-sac, Kingsdown Mount.

2. At the top of the rise turn left to end of cul-de-sac and pass between two fences, on the right between Nos. 30 and 32, on to a track, tarmac at first, then earth, going up a low hill. We are now entering Bramcote Hills (B).

3. Keep straight on, ignoring a right and a left turn, following the fencing on the right.

4. At a path junction near the top of the hill, by footpath signs, turn right along clear track, passing a housing estate on the left, for about 250 metres. Keep right of the footpath sign on the hilltop, then go straight on for 150 metres to meet a road (Markham Road).

5. Go straight along Markham Road for about 100 metres to a T-junction with another road (Sandy Lane).

6. Turn right along Sandy Lane to the end of the cul-de-sac and continue ahead along a well-marked bridleway which shortly bears left. Ignore a track to the right and continue leftwards to reach Thoresby Road (going uphill towards your left).

7. Cross Thoresby Road and pass to right of car park of Bramcote Hills Golf Course, along a signposted footpath between fences.

8. On reaching a road (Deddington Lane) by a footpath sign, turn left along the pavement, with houses on the other side of the road.

9. Where Deddington Lane bears right to become Eastcote Avenue, keep straight ahead along a pleasant tree-lined track with Golf Course on the left.

10. After 700 metres reach a T-junction with a wider track. Here turn left uphill.

21. At a footpath sign turn right, going between fence of a School and hawthorn hedge. Follow this for 200 metres to reach a stile.

22. On reaching a chain-link fence turn left uphill towards woodland, along t|| right-hand side of the sports field.

23. Enter the wood and take diagonal path to the right, going uphill.

24. Bear right again after 70 metres to follow boundary fence to a quarry c right. Keep parallel to the fence and take a left turn where the path straig| ahead appears to drop steeply downhill. The path we follow drops down to t| Car Park in Bramcote Park (B).

REFRESHMENTS

Bramcote Manor Inn   Moor Farm. Coventry Lane. Bar meals. Snacks.

INTEREST

A. WOLLATON HALL   Formerly the home of the Willoughby family, whic| includes in its numbers a Lord Chief Justice, a famous navigator and a famou| naturalist, the Hall, built in 1580–1588, is one of the finest Elizabethan building| in England, distinguished for its (apparent)] symmetry and its raised centra| hall. It is owned, like the Park in which it stands, by the City of Nottingham, an| is now a Natural History Museum. The Museum is open daily except o| Christmas Day, and admission is free except on Sundays and Bank Holidays| when there is a small charge. For current admission times, please enquire from| the Museum or the Nottingham Information Bureau. The Hall gardens ar| lovely, and a special feature is the early 19th-century cast-iron Camellia House| which recently narrowly escaped total dereliction, following a public appeal fo| funds to carry out its restoration.

The Stables, just down the hill from the hall, are now the City of Nottingham| Industrial Museum, which boasts some very fine exhibits from Nottingham'| industrial history, especially lace and printing. There is a mid-19th-century beam| engine, which is 'in steam' on the last Sunday in each month. Admission detail| are as for the Natural History Museum.

Wollaton Park   This fine Park is hilly country is perhaps the most popula|

open space within the City limits, with its noble trees, its Lake – a Mecca for anglers – , its many pleasant walks, its Golf Course, and its superb half-kilometre long lime grove to the Hall from the Middleton Boulevard entrance (prohibited to motor vehicles). The Park has been the venue for military tattoos, Scout Jamborees, Agricultural Shows, and many other events, and has attractions at all seasons. Herds of fallow and red deer roam the grounds. The brick wall enclosing the Park dates originally from the 17th century. The Park, with the Hall, was originally nearly 800 acres in extent, and when the whole estate was sold to the Nottingham Corporation in 1925, 528 acres remained as parkland, the rest being sold for housing development. Thereby the Corporation recovered the whole of the purchase price of the estate! There is a Nature Trail around the Lake. The Park is open daily **until dusk** and there is ample car-parking, as well as toilet and refreshment facilities.

B. BRAMCOTE PARK Bramcote Hills and the associated area of open space known as Bramcote Park form one of the most important recreational assets in the southern part of Broxtowe District. Over recent years it has been much encroached upon by housing developments and it is hoped that what remains of the attractive tree-clad sandstone hills will be left as a Green Belt area. At present there is a public golf course, a beautiful park at Bramcote, and projected plans to create a dry ski-slope in the disused part of the sand workings off Coventry Lane. The route of the Robin Hood Way to the Nottingham Canal (see Section 3) via Stapleford Hill is part of a new recreational route set up by the District Council.

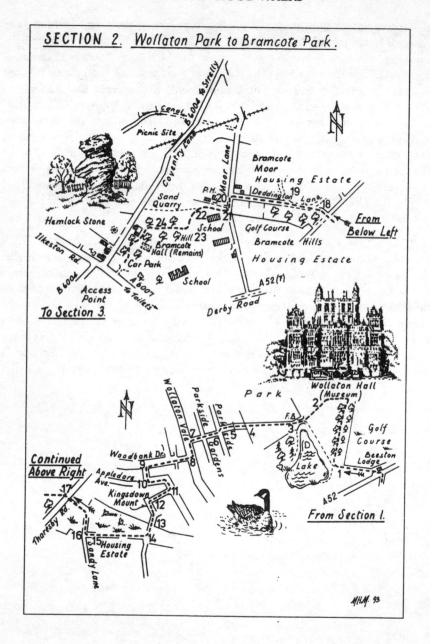

SECTION 2. Wollaton Park to Bramcote Park.

3. BRAMCOTE PARK TO KIMBERLEY

Distance: 8 km. (5 miles.)

Maps: Landranger Sheet 129.   1:25,000 Series Sheets SK.53, SK.43, SK.44 & SK. 54.

Start: Bramcote Park Car Park.

How to get there: Follow the A.52 (Nottingham to Derby Road) to the large lights-controlled junction opposite the Sherwin Arms Public House, taking the outside lane at the approach to the junction, then take the A.6007. Turn first right off this road on to the A.6002 (Coventry Lane). The Car Park is a short distance along Coventry Lane, on the right-hand side.

For public transport services, telephone the 'Bus Hotline' (Nottm. 240000).

THE ROUTE

1. Cross Coventry Lane from the Car Park and turn right for 100 metres to reach a stile.

2. By a sign for the Hemlock Stone turn left and take the path going uphill to the Hemlock Stone (A).

3. On reaching the Stone it is now possible to gain an interesting view of 3 counties by walking from the Stone, following waymark signs to reach the summit trig point of Stapleford Hill. After admiring the view retrace your steps to the Stone, then follow the footpath sign from the Stone and contour around Stapleford Hill along lower path, to reach the edge of a wooded area. Go through scrub land with iron railings seen to the right, to enter the corner of a field.

4. Cross this field corner and in 10 metres go through a gap in willow trees, turn left and follow the edge of a field to a stile (**). Turn left and walk along a path in a cluster of trees to reach a junction. Turn right and climb uphill, then left to eventually reach a gate and a car park. (Alternative route at (**). Cross stile and climb staircase opposite, to follow a wide sandy track above the railway, eventually reaching a gate and car park.)

5. DO NOT go through the gate, but turn right and follow the path between fences, cross the railway carefully, go over a stile and bear left across a field to a stile leading to the perimeter fence of a Garden Centre which straddles the disused Nottingham Canal (B).

6. Turn left along perimeter fence.

7. Pass by the entrance to the Garden Centre, going slightly left to cross a narrow road at a signpost 'Public Footpath to Swansea Bridge'. Cross the road and continue in the same direction for a short distance, with hedge on right, then turn right with the hedge. The busy M1 is now visible to your left.

8. Go over a stile, still curving right and dropping slightly to a brick and stone bridge over the canal. This is Swansea Bridge.

9. On the far side of the bridge take stile to left of the gate with a Public Footpath sign pointing left. Go along the canal bank to another stile.

10. Go over this stile and curve slightly right, following the outside edge of a thicket, with barbed wire to your right and the canal through the trees to your left.

11. After about 550 metres there is a junction of fences with two stiles. DO NOT take the one opposite, which leads to Trowell (C), but take the one to the right, crossing a field with a fence to your left, passing by the end of a power line, to reach a stile with another sign for a footpath to Swansea Bridge.

12. Go over the stile and bear slightly left to a five-barred gate and on to a road (A.609, Nottingham Road, Trowell). To your left there is a telephone kiosk in a lay-by.

13. Turn right along the road for about 300 metres, using the opposite pavement, as far as a road to the left, Waterloo Lane, with a 'No Entry' sign and another saying 'Private Road', behind which, in the hedge, is a bridleway sign and waymark to Strelley and Cossall.

14. Turn down Waterloo Lane, heading towards the M1 Service Station.

15. Where Waterloo Lane bends left towards the Service Station, there is a bridleway sign in the hedge on the right. Go through the bridlegate at this sign and turn left along the field edge for about 100 metres.

16. After 100 metres the path turns slightly left between some trees and up some steps leading into another field. Follow the headland of this field with a hedge on right, rising gently to pass under a small power line which goes to a farm on the hill to your right.

17. Shortly after this, the path curves slightly right, going through a gap in the crossing hedge and continuing slightly uphill towards a spinney – Shaw's Plantation.

18. Just before the spinney, by a fence, is a bridlegate. Here a bridleway between Cossall and Balloon Woods crosses our route. (This bridleway makes a short cut from Coventry Lane and Deddington Lane in Section 1 point 19, and also leads to an interesting circular walk.) Cross this bridleway and continue straight ahead towards Strelley.

19. On reaching the spinney, go through a bridlegate to the right of it and continue in the same direction, with the spinney on your left, along field-headlands. To the right are fine views of Nottingham, with Wollaton Hall prominent in the middle distance.

20. After crossing several fields by bridlegates, come to a T-junction with a wide track. Strelley Lane. DO NOT turn left, but descend slightly to take bridle road to the left between hedges, passing a fine group of beech trees. Ignore a later track to the left.

21. After about 250 metres, when Strelley Hall and Church become visible straight ahead, the bridle road curves right to reach the road, Main Street, running through the village of Strelley (D). (Refreshments available at the pub in the village.)

22. Turn left along the road, passing Strelley Church and Hall. Go past the first public footpath to the left after the church and continue to reach the buildings of Home Farm on the left.

23. Pass between wooden posts by a sign 'Public Footpath and Bridleway, Swingate', and continue ahead to a cottage, Holly Cottage. Turn left across the bridge over the M1. (Be careful, the bridge will only carry one vehicle at a time!)

24. At the far side turn left along a rough track for about 100 metres, at which point the track turns right by the side of a hedge. A TV mast and a water tower now appear ahead near the top of a slight rise.

25. After passing a cottage (Bridlepath Cottage) to your left, go between a hedge and a fence, towards the tower.

26. At the end of the next field join a wide track and continue between tower and mast to some houses and a tarmac road.

27. Where this road bears right, keep ahead along a narrow track between hedges to reach the Queen Adelaide Inn.

28. At the Inn turn left for a few metres, cross the road and take another path by the side of railings, passing the water tower and a covered reservoir, taking several turns around the perimeter fence.

29. When the perimeter fence swings left and a wooden fence leads down to the right, turn right along the wooden fence to emerge on to a street at a footpath sign. This is Spring Hill.

30. Turn left past Kimberley Close to the end of Spring Hill, then take a public footpath going straight on across a large field, to reach a stile on the right, partly hidden through a hedge. Go over the stile and walk straight ahead, keeping to the high ground, to a further F.P. sign.

31. Turn right and head for a stile at the side of the by-pass road. Go over the stile and turn right to take an underpass. Now turn left and walk parallel to the road to reach the junction of the path with the steel boundary fencing of a Council Depot. Go around this perimeter fencing, ignoring a stile on the left, then take a track through a gap in a former railway to reach Eastwood Road, Kimberley.

REFRESHMENTS

'Broad Oak' Inn, Strelley   Meals.
'Queen Adelaide' Inn, Swingate   Snacks.

INTEREST

A. HEMLOCK STONE This isolated 31 ft. high outcrop of red sandstone has been protected from the weathering effect of the atmosphere by its capping of harder, pebbly stone. It has legendary associations with religious rites, especially the cult of fire and sun worship.

B. NOTTINGHAM CANAL This Canal originally ran from Trent Bridge to the Cromford Canal at Langley Mill, a distance of 14¾ miles, and was completed in 1777. The section from Lenton was closed in 1936 and has since been filled-in in places. Other parts are overgrown, particularly the stretch from Coventry Lane to the Garden Centre, though Broxtowe District Council are considering developing this stretch for recreational purposes.

C. TROWELL This village was chosen as Britain's 'Festival Village' in 1951 during the Festival of Britain, which commemorated the Centenary of the Great Exhibition of 1851 at Crystal Palace, London. It was chosen as a fine example of a village coming to terms with agriculture on one side and industry on the other – collieries and ironworks. It has an interesting old church which has in its tower the works of the old clock which used to stand in the biggest open market-place in England – the Market Square in Nottingham. The village is now 'flown over' by the M1 Motorway. .

D. STRELLEY This peaceful unspoilt village has interesting old cottages and a tree-lined main street, a pub (The Broad Oak), but no shops. It is now a Conservation Area. From Norman times until the days of Charles II the De Stradlegh family lived here and their tombs are in the church, which also contains many fine examples of carving in alabaster and a particularly well-preserved Rood Screen. Strelley Hall, rebuilt in 1789 and standing in a pleasant park, was owned by the De Stradleghs until 1651, when the estate was sold to a lawyer, Ralph Edge, whose family kept possession of the Hall until the death of the last Miss Edge, in 1978. It is now used for business purposes.

E. KIMBERLEY This is an industrial village which has only grown since 1816. Its most famous product at present is Kimberley Ale. There used to be two stations here in this one village; one on the Midland Line, closed in 1951, the other on the Northern Line was closed in 1964.

COSSALL AND COSSALL MARSH Though not on the direct route of the Robin Hood Way, Cossall is included in one of the associated circular walks, and is well worth a visit. This is a delightful rural area in the midst of collieries, where the first Notts. coal was dug as long ago as 1316. There are some fine old buildings in Cossall, including Church Cottage, the home of the fiancée of the novelist D.H. Lawrence, who wrote about the village in 'The Rainbow'. Also worthy of note are the Willoughby Almshouses, the Waterloo Memorial and the partly 13th-century church, containing a fine oak reredos, made by the village carvers.

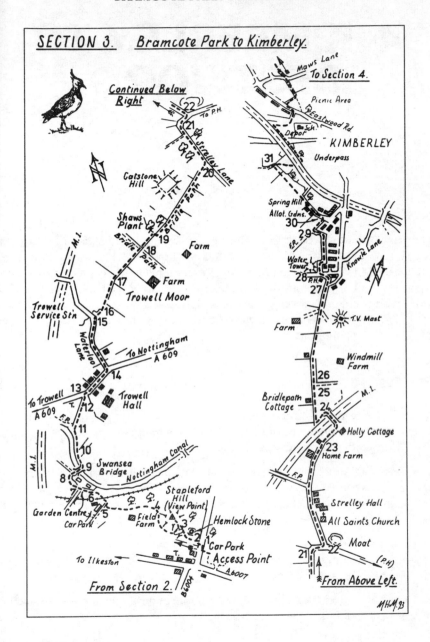

SECTION 3.   Bramcote Park to Kimberley.

4. KIMBERLEY TO BESTWOOD

Distance: 10 km. (6.25 miles).

Maps: Landranger Sheet 129.   1:25,000 Series Sheet SK.54.

Start: Eastwood Road, Kimberley.

How to get there: By road: leave Nottingham by the A.610 (Alfreton Road). At the large island at Nuthall, where the link road to the M.1 is signed, bear right on B.600 and follow signs to Kimberley. Descend hill in Kimberley, passing War Memorial and Supermarket on left. Eastwood Road is the continuation of the main road through Kimberley. There are signposted car parks in Station Road. By public transport: For bus services from Nottingham enquire from the 'Bus Hotline', Tel. Nottm. 240000.

THE ROUTE

1. Cross Eastwood Road, turn left and walk to a stile in the hedge. Enter an open space (Hall Om Wong) and walk uphill to a footpath between two houses. Follow this path through to Maws Lane.

2. Cross road and continue along Edinboro Row and walk past the front of houses to take a footpath to a further open space. This was the former site of two windmills. Ignore footpaths at a junction but carry straight on to a stile into an open field.

3. Go over this stile into the field, turn right and aim for a large tree by a gap in a hedge. Go through the gap and in the next field drop down to the far corner to a further stile, then go straight on across two fields to arrive at the Gilt Brook.

4. DO NOT go over the bridge over the brook, but turn right and walk along the side of the Gilt Brook to the next crossing.

5. Go over bridge and stile and cross field diagonally to the left to a stile into the next field, then go straight on to the next stile. DO NOT cross this stile but turn right and aim for Greasley Church, seen ahead. Now walk to Greasley Church (A), crossing over six stiles.

6. Retrace your steps to the third stile at a path junction. Do not cross this stile, but turn left and follow field edge path, with hedge on right, to another stile.

7. Cross over farm track to stile opposite, then follow the path across two fields to rejoin Gilt Brook at a junction of three paths.

8. Go over stile, then over concrete bridge and over a further stile, then climb the hill for 40 metres to a further stile on right.

9. Go over this stile, turn left and climb to top of field.

10. Go over a stile and follow track around a cottage, then take footpath on right, signposted to Watnall.

11. Follow the track through the wood, ignoring all detours, to arrive at a stile and farm track.

12. Go over stile and cross farm track to another stile opposite, then continue across Rolleston Park, first climbing, then going over crest of hill, aiming slightly right, to reach a path junction.

13. Turn left and take path downhill into Watnall. Go over a stile, then through a gap in a fence into a wooded area. Follow the path through the plantation to a further stile.

14. Turn left on Trough Road and walk to road junction (Watnall Road B.600). Refreshments are available at the Queen's Head.

15. Cross the road and take path opposite, firstly along a narrow path, then into a field. Go across three fields in a straight line to reach railway line. Go over this and across a further field to the side of the M.1. Turn left and walk up field edge to a road (Long Lane).

16. Turn right and walk over M.1 bridge towards a bus shelter, then take a bridleway on right signposted to Hucknall.

17 Halfway across the second field turn left towards Bulwell Wood (B).

18. Go through a gate and follow path until another path comes in from right.

19. At this junction continue along the perimeter of Hucknall Airfield (C) on a well-marked path.

20. When farm buildings appear on the left (Woodhall Farm), go through a gate on the main farm drive and, ignoring the turn into the farm, continue along the airfield boundary.

21. At a corner of the airfield, by some meteorological equipment, continue one field further, then turn left on a clear track. Pass through a gap with an old brick 'pillbox' just through to the right, and continue with the airfield on your left and a hedge on the right. After about 100 metres the hedge is replaced by a row of fence posts. (Take care along here – there is a public golf course on your right. KEEP TO THE WAYMARKED PATH – DO NOT DISTURB THE GOLFERS!)

22. Soon the direct path peters out. Now bear slightly right towards a hawthorn hedgerow forming the boundary of the nurseries at Bulwell Hall (D). Keep to this hedge, following it round to a track with a row of yew trees on the left, then to meet a tarmac road leading up to the Hall.

23. Turn right on this road, with a holly hedge on left, as far as a new Sports Pavilon with Car Park.

24. Go around this Pavilion to resume the previous line of the route.

25. Take the track going straight ahead and follow this for about 200 metres with a plantation and wire fence on your left, eventually to arrive at another junction.

26. Turn right at this point and follow the track to arrive at an old cart-bridge. Cross this and then turn right. After a further 250 metres the track turns left and heads towards a disused railway line.

27. Pass through a gap in the old railway line and then go in a rightish direction along a clear bridleway which reaches a road after about 700 metres.

28. Turn left along the road (Nottingham Road) for 80 metres, towards an island, then cross the road and take a signposted path over a railway line and go past mill buildings to meet another road (Moor Road).

REFRESHMENTS

Queen's Head, Watnall   Bar meals.
'Golden Guinea', junction of Maws Lane and Cornfield Road, Kimberley Snacks.

INTEREST

A. GREASLEY   A village in the mining area, its 15th century church stands high on a hilltop and is a landmark for miles around. Here once existed Greasley Castle, the fortified manor house of the Cantilupe family, begun around 1341. All that remains are a few humps and hollows near Castle Farm – the scant remains of the former moat.

B. BULWELL WOOD   This is one of several Sites of Special Scientific interest met along the Way. Bulwell Wood Hall was the home of some of the Byron family.

C. HUCKNALL AIRFIELD   This is a former R.A.F. station, now the property of Rolls Royce Limited. It has been the scene of the testing of a number of developments in aircraft construction which have historical significance. One of the best-known was the 'Flying Bedstead', the first vertical take-off aircraft, which flew in 1954. (A local pub has bene named after it.) The airfield was also the scene of a famous escape attempt in 1940, when Franz von Werra, a German prisoner-of-war, attempted to steal a Hurricane fighter.

D. BULWELL HALL   The Hall was built in 1770 by John Newton and was once derisively known as Pye-Wipe Hall. The last private owner was Alderman Ball, the father of Albert Ball V.C., the famous World War I pilot. He sold it to Nottingham Corporation, and it was demolished in 1958. The public Golf Course in the park was opened in 1910. Refreshments may be found in the summer at the Bulwell entrance to the Park, where there are also toilets.

ROBIN HOOD'S WELL & BEAUVALE PRIORY   The remains of Beauvale Priory are visible from the B.600 road, a little further along from Greasley. It was founded in 1343 by Nicholas de Cantelupe, a great soldier and friend of Edward III and is, therefore, contemporary with the Cantelupe (or Cantilupe) family's castle at Greasley. Robin Hood's Well is situated in High Park Wood behind the Priory ruins. Both these sites are on PRIVATE LAND with NO public access.

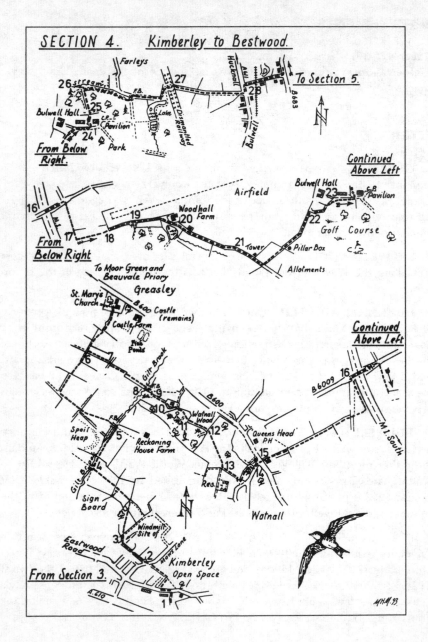

SECTION 4.   Kimberley to Bestwood.

Farleys

26 stream
27
Hucknall
A611
To Section 5.

28
B683

F.B.
25
Lake
Dismantled Railway

Bulwell Hall
C.P.
Pavilion
Park

24

Bulwell

From Below Right.

Continued Above Left

Bulwell Hall
23
C.P. Pavilion

16
Airfield
19
Woodhall Farm
20
22
Golf Course

17
18
21 Tower
Pillar Box

From Below Right
Allotments

To Moor Green and
Beauvale Priory
Greasley

St. Mary's Church
B600 Castle (remains)

Castle Farm

Continued Above Left

Fish Ponds

Gilt Brook

6
B6009 16
M.1. South

8
F.B.
B600

10
Watnall Wood

Spoil Heap
5
Reckoning House Farm
11
12
Queens Head P.H.

15

4
13
Res.

Gilt Brook

Sign Board
Watnall

N

Windmill Site of

Eastwood Road
3
Mans Lane

2
Kimberley Open Space

From Section 3.
A.610

1

M.H.M. 93.

5. BESTWOOD TO BURNTSTUMP PARK

Distance: 11 Km. (6.9 miles.)

Maps: Landranger Sheets 129 and 120.   1:25,000 Series Sheet SK.54 & SK.55.

Start: Bestwood Village (Moor Road). The nearest car parking is at the Winding House Car Park of Bestwood Country Park (on Park Road, Bestwood).

How to get there: By Road, take A.611 ([Hucknall Road) from Nottingham. After passing Bulwell Forest Golf Course, turn right at lights just before a bridge over a railway, on to B.683 (Bestwood and Papplewick). This is Moor Road. Continue into Bestwood and turn right on to Park Road, the first right turn.

By public transport: For local bus services, enquire from the 'Bus Hotline', Tel. Nottm. 240000.

THE ROUTE

1. If following on from Section 4, on reaching Moor Road, turn left and follow the road to a bend where a disused railway line reached the road (the bridge has been removed). (If coming from Winding House Car Park, walk back along Park Road to the junction with Moor Road, turn left along Moor Road and walk to the sign for Mill Lakes, then pick up the route.)

2. 250 metres further on, on the far side of a railway embankment, step over the low wall on your left (signed Mill Lakes), ascend steps up the embankment, then bear right to enter Bestwood Country Park (A) at a footbridge over the River Leen.

3. There is now a choice of routes across this part of the Park.

3a. One is to cross the bridge and follow the path leading up a low hill, then going right, along a clear track along the ridge with a plantation to left. Later this track bears right again and drops to a gate, leading to a narrow tarmac road, along which turn right. THIS IS THE RECOMMENDED ROUTE, as it gives better views of the Lake.

3b. The other route is to turn right just before the footbridge and follow a clear winding track beside the Lake. This eventually crosses a field towards a house in the top right-hand corner, beside which is a gate leading to the narrow tarmac road reached in 3a.

From both these alternatives, follow the narrow road to its junction with B.683 opposite a telephone kiosk.

4. Turn left along B.683, crossing the road, then almost immediately turn right along a street called The Spinney. Follow this street round until you see the end of the cul-de-sac.

5. Just before the end of the street, turn left on to a signposted path between houses. This path then climbs with a hedge on left. Continue along tarmac path over a stile and across two fields to a road. Turn left and continue along the road, bearing right to enter the main Bestwood Country Park and eventually reach Alexandra Lodge (B).

6. Pass the Lodge on its left-hand side, ignore a side turn and continue on a sandy track climbing a hill (Violet Hill) and along a former colliery path to meet a clear track at the top. At this point a right turn would take you to Bestwood Lodge, where refreshments are available.

7. Turn left and follow the wide track which passes through a gate and then becomes metalled where a road joins from the right.

8. Continue ahead along the metalled track in the same direction to the entrance to a caravan park.

9. Bear left at this entrance, going downhill to the gateway to Boarding Kennels.

10. Turn left at this gateway and continue along the same track, ignoring all side turns but bearing steadily left. After passing a Sports Ground to the right continue along track to rejoin B.683.

11. Turn right along B.683, go under railway bridge, and pass the Lido.

12. After about 1½ km. (0.9 miles) along the road, opposite a road to Hucknall and Linby (C), turn right over a stile along a signposted footpath to Seven Mile House and Calverton. Follow this path across several fields, aiming for the farm on the horizon (Stanker Hill Farm).

13. At the farm, enter the compound and go round to the right of the buildings on to a track which passes through a gate and over a stile, then runs alongside a railway embankment and through a plantation to reach the A.60 Nottingham to Mansfield Road.

14. Turn right along the A.60 as far as Seven Mile House, then cross the road and turn left along a minor road.

15. Follow this road for about 200 metres and turn right at the signed entrance to Burntstump Park (D), Park Hospital and Notts. County Police H.Q. Follow the entrance road until you see a path on its left-hand side, in the trees. This leads into the Car Park (toilets and refreshments).

REFRESHMENTS

Bestwood Hotel, Bestwood Park   Bar meals, restaurant.

'Griffin's Head', Papplewick crossroads   Bar meals.

Seven Mile House, on A.60 opposite minor road to Burntstump Park   Licensed restaurant.

Burntstump Inn, Burntstump Park   Bar meals.

INTEREST

A. BESTWOOD COUNTRY PARK   The first part of this Park, around the Mill Lakes, is a recent development which includes attractive short walks, new plantations, a Lake with wildfowl, a peat-bog (a rare find in the heart of Notts.) and a proposed Nature Reserve for Schools, all built on a former domestic rubbish tip and bisected by the River Leen, which has been dammed to create the Lake. The major part of the Park originally consisted of 4000 unfenced acres of Sherwood Forest, was mentioned in Domesday Book, and has been connected with royalty since 1160. It was lent to nobility and gentry for centuries, and in 1683 was granted to Nell Gwynne's illegitimate son, the first Duke of St. Alban's, and remained in the possession of successive Dukes until it was sold in 1938. During this time the Estate was one of the most brilliant social centres in the country. In more recent years it has been disturbed by coal-mining, but the former tip has been grassed over and the Park is gradually regaining its country appearance. Bestwood Lodge, within the Park and now a Hotel, was built by the 10th Duke on the site of a former hunting lodge. It has statues of some of the Sherwood Forest outlaws, similar to those to be found later along the Robin Hood Way at Archway House, and is one of the best examples in Notts. of the High Victorian mansion in a lavish style, but of medium size.

B. ALEXANDRA LODGE This Lodge at the entrance to Bestwood Park lay disused for several years and has now been skilfully renovated after being vandalised, and has been turned into an Information Centre and a Ranger Centre for the Park.

C. LINBY The village, lying just off our route, ought to be visited by those interested in the history and architecture of the area. It is one of the few mainly stone-built villages in Notts., thanks to the Magnesian Limestone which is quarried here. The two streams flowing on either side of the main street are not only attractive, but were used to provide power for the local mills, which at first were corn mills, only later being used to produce cotton. There are some attractive cottages in the village, which has managed not to be completely spoiled by the proximity of the collieries.

D. BURNTSTUMP PARK This is another attractive area which has been opened as a Country Park, this time by the Gedling District Council. Just to the right of the entrance is Sherwood Lodge, formerly owned by the National Coal Board and now the Headquarters of Notts. County Police, whilst to the left is the recently built Park Hospital. The Burntstump Inn will be found snugly set in the far side of the Park. Burntstump Park is an ideal place for a short walk followed by a visit to the Inn.

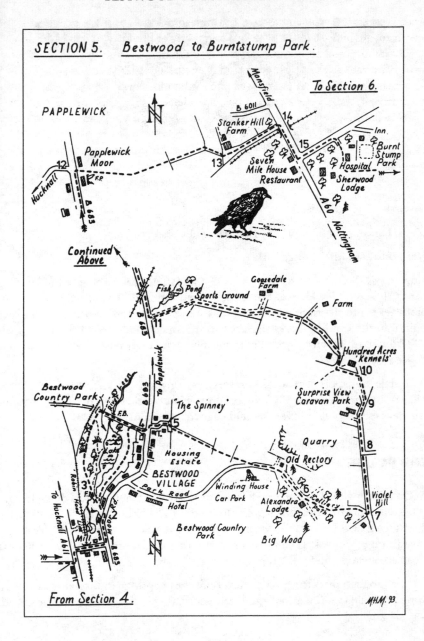

SECTION 5. *Bestwood to Burntstump Park.*

To Section 6.

PAPPLEWICK

N

B 6011

Stanker Hill Farm

Papplewick Moor

Seven Mile House Restaurant

Inn

Burnt Stump Park

Hospital

Sherwood Lodge

Hucknall

12

F.P.

13

14

15

A 683

Mansfield

A 60

Nottingham

Continued Above

Fish Pond

Sports Ground

Goosedale Farm

Farm

B 683

11

Hundred Acres 'Kennels'

10

Bestwood Country Park

F.B.

To Papplewick

B 683

'The Spinney'

'Surprise View Caravan Park

9

River Leen

Lake

4

5

Housing Estate

BESTWOOD VILLAGE

Quarry

Old Rectory

8

To Hucknall

3

Robin Hood Way

F.

Park Road

Winding House Car Park

Colliery Path

6

Alexandra Lodge

Violet Hill

7

Hotel

Mill

2

A 683

1

N

Bestwood Country Park

Big Wood

6. BURNTSTUMP PARK TO BLIDWORTH

Distance: 8 km. (5 miles.)

Maps: Landranger Sheet 120.   1:25,000 Series Sheet SK55.

Start: Burntstump Country Park.

How to get there: By road, take the A.60 (Mansfield) road going out of Nottingham. At Seven Mile House, about 3 km. from the traffic island where the A.614 branches off to the right, turn right on a minor road, and after 200 metres turn right into the Country Park (signposted). It can also be reached from the A.614 (Ollerton road) by turning left down the minor road signposted 'Papplewick and Police Headquarters.'

By public transport: For local bus services, ring the 'Bus Hotline' on Nottm. 240000. In summer, the 'Sherwood Forester' network visits the Park on some journeys (see separate advertisement page in this Guide.)

THE ROUTE

1. On reaching the Car Park, take the path above it, with the toilets down to your left, and follow this clear track going to the top right-hand corner of the Park and through a gate on to a track passing a Sports Ground on your right, and continue ahead along this track. (There are other paths in the Country Park – if any of these are used, always aim for the top corner.)

2. At a junction of paths, do not turn right, but continue in the same direction, along a metalled track which passes Seely Church School and goes out on to a road.

. Turn left along this road for about 75 metres.

. Turn right down a rough track, passing two houses on your left, and going downhill for 600 metres to meet a minor road.

. Continue ahead along the verge of the minor road, passing Papplewick Pumping Station (A) after 750 metres, and reach a crossroads. (Up the road to the left at this crossroads, some 5 minutes walk away, is Longdale Craft Centre – shop, toilets and refreshments.)

. Turn right at the crossroads and use the verge along the road, under trees. After 100 metres, on the left-hand side of this road (Longdale Lane), there is a sign at the start of a permissive forest track that keeps by the hedgerow just inside a plantation. This plantation is used to rear game birds and is therefore a sensitive area – please keep strictly to the track at all times. After 800 metres this track reaches the Longdale Lane picnic site and car park (B).

7. Turn left into the car park, go through the parking area, past a pole barrier and into the plantation along a broad track, climbing steadily.

8. After about 1.5 km., at a major track junction, go half right, dropping downhill to reach Blidworth Bottoms Car Park (toilets).

9. Go past a pole barrier on to the road (Blidworth Lane) and turn left.

10. At the first house on the right, turn right up a sandy bridleway (Beck Lane) and follow this for about 1200 metres to the top of the hill, ignoring all side turns, to reach a junction with a tarmac road.

11. Continue ahead along this road, downhill, to its junction with the main road, near Blidworth Well (C) on your right.

12. Turn left along this road into Blidworth (D), as far as the road junction by the Black Bull Public House.

12a. Make a detour from the route by continuing along the main road past the Black Bull, as far as Blidworth Church (E), then return to the Black Bull.

REFRESHMENTS

Burntstump Inn, Burntstump Park   Bar meals.

Black Bull, Blidworth   Bar meals.

Bird in Hand, Blidworth   Bar meals (not Sundays).

INTEREST

A. PAPPLEWICK PUMPING STATION   Constructed in 1883–5, having been originally built to pump water from the porous sandstone for Nottingham, it is no longer in service, but the site has been developed into a museum of power production. The building features a pair of beam engines built by James Watt now preserved in working order by enthusiasts and put under steam with the use of six Lancashire boilers, some ornate Victorian architecture and elaborate internal decoration. Note also the working forge and large cooling pond in landscaped grounds. Open to the public from Easter to the end of October.

B. LONGDALE LANE PICNIC SITE   This is one of several recently opened to the public by the Forestry Commission. There are numerous waymarked tracks through the woods, including some circular routes.

C. BLIDWORTH WELL   The well has recently been replaced in its original place, after having spent some years in a museum. It is now 'dressed' annually by local children, in a similar way to many Peak District wells.

D. BLIDWORTH   (Pronounced locally 'Blidduth'). A mining village with an ancient hill fortress and 'barrows'. Also in the vicinity is the 'Druid Stone', a pillar of pebbly rock left behind by the retreating glacier in the Ice Ages. A footpath from the village passes close by it. Blidworth is in the heart of the Sherwood Forest area and has associations with Robin Hood. This is the village from which Robin Hood took his bride Maid Marian to be married at Edwinstowe. It has several pubs, as well as shops. It is of interest that the Dover Beck was in mediaeval times a navigable river from the River Trent as far as Blidworth Bottoms, but is now only a small stream.

E. BLIDWORTH CHURCH   This modern church with a 15th century tower dominates the village. In the churchyard there purports to be the grave of Will Scarlet, one of Robin Hood's band. The principal claim to fame of the church is the Rocking Ceremony, performed on the first Sunday in February. The last baby boy to have been baptised is dedicated at the altar and rocked in a cradle in the sanctuary. His name is then recorded in the Register of Rockings. The ceremony was observed in olden days as a simple miracle play, representing the taking of Jesus to the Temple.

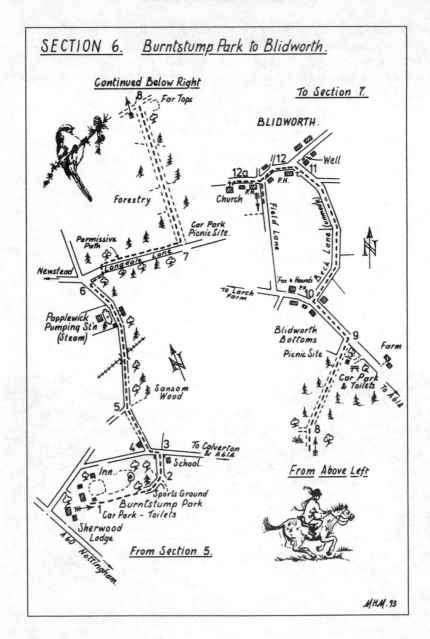

SECTION 6.   Burntstump Park to Blidworth.

Continued Below Right

8 ... Far Tops

To Section 7.

BLIDWORTH.

12

Well

12a

11

P.H.

Church

Forestry

Field Lane

Beck Lane (unmade)

Car Park Picnic Site.

Permissive Path

Longdale Lane

7

Newstead

6

To Larch Farm

Fox & Hounds P.H.

10

Papplewick Pumping Stn (Steam)

Blidworth Bottoms Picnic Site

9

Farm

Car Park & Toilets

To A614

Sansom Wood

5

8

4   3

To Calverton & A614

School.

From Above Left

2

Sports Ground

Inn..

Burntstump Park

1   Car Park - Toilets

Sherwood Lodge

A60 Nottingham.

From Section 5.

M.H.M. 93

34

7. BLIDWORTH TO NOMANSHILL WOOD

Distance: 10 km. (6.25 miles).

Maps: Landranger Sheet 120.   1:25,000 Series Sheet SK.55.

Start: Blidworth, Black Bull Public House. (Street parking in Blidworth).

How to get there: By road – from the A.60 at Ravenshead, or the A.617 at Rainworth, take the B.6020 leading into Blidworth.

By public transport: For local bus services, ring the 'Bus Hotline' on Nottm. 240000.

THE ROUTE

1. If coming from Section 6, at the Black Bull turn left down Field Lane (this is a right turn when returning from the church) and go downhill for about 200 metres to reach a footpath sign on the right.

2. At the footpath sign turn right, over a stile, and cross to a second stile.

3. Bear slightly left for two fields.

4. Go straight across several narrow fields, one of which is divided into allotment gardens.

NB. There may be loose horses in some of these fields, and care should be taken.

5. On reaching a large field, cross it, aiming for a brick building with a tower to the right side, reaching a footpath sign in the hedge at the side of a road.

6. Turn left at the road, passing the telephone exchange on your right, and go a right-hand bend in the road.

7. Do not go right with the road at this bend, but continue straight ahead along a wide track signposted to Kighill and Papplewick for about 1.5 km. to emerge a road junction opposite a petrol station.

8. Take the road opposite, to the right of the petrol station (Kighill Lane), as far as its junction with the main road A.60.

9. Cross A.60 and go over a stile on to a signposted path (to Papplewick) with hedge on right, to a small copse, where you bear left to the edge of a wood.

10. Go left outside the wood, then turn right into the wood on a clear track.

11. At the far side of the wood turn left to a T-junction of tracks by a hedge.

12. Turn right at hedge and follow it along a line of pylons to a gate leading on to a road.

13. Turn left down this rather narrow road, downhill, keeping on the right hand side round a right-hand bend, to the gates of Papplewick Hall (A). Just before this point you pass the site of Robin Hood's Stables (B).

NB. Take extreme care along this narrow road and beware of fast traffic.

14. At the footpath signpost to Larch Farm turn right along a broad track leading from the road. This bends right, then goes straight for 1.2 km. to the iron gates at the entrance to Newstead Abbey Estate.

15. Go through the side gate by the lodge (South Lodge) and continue ahead along the metalled drive for a further 1 km. (Newstead Abbey is visible to the left.)

16. Where the drive bends to the left, keep straight ahead along a path through trees and after 50 metres drop down to cross the main drive into Newstead Abbey (C).

NOTE: There is a charge for entrance to Newstead Abbey grounds and there are notices indicating that there is no public entry from the footpath, which crosses the main drive.

17. Cross the main drive and continue in the same direction through trees, at first uphill, then dropping steeply into a small valley with a wall on the right. In view, slightly to the left, is Newstead Hospital. This attractive path is known locally as 'Up the ladder and over the wall'.

18. Shortly after passing the hospital, at a stile, go left for a few metres, then right between hedges, to emerge on to a road, B.6020.

19. Turn left at this road and after 100 metres turn right down a side road signposted Sutton-in-Ashfield.

20. At the foot of the slight hill, by a small lay-by on the right, take the signposted footpath into Nomanshill Wood. (Access Car Park is on the right a little further along the road, and is signed 'Thieves Wood Car Park'.)

REFRESHMENTS

Black Bull, Blidworth   Bar meals.

Bird in Hand, Blidworth   Bar meals (not Sundays).

INTEREST

A. PAPPLEWICK HALL   The Hall was designed by the Adam brothers for Sir Frederick Montagu, Lord of the Treasury, in 1787. A worth-while detour is to Papplewick village, which is of Saxon origin. The cotton mills here originated a major English industry, until they were closed and partly demolished by local landowners in the 19th century. Papplewick Church, which has a 400-year old yew tree, is where Robin Hood's minstrel, Alan-A-Dale, was married by Little John.

B. ROBIN HOOD'S STABLES   A well-hidden cave in the sandstone near the Lodge of Papplewick Hall, is said to be the place where Robin hid his horses when visiting Nottingham. It is on private land.

** Permission to view may be obtained **in advance only** by S.A.E. and written application to The Occupier, Re Robin Hood's Stables, The Hermitage, Blidworth Waye, Papplewick, Nottingham NG15 8EP.

C. NEWSTEAD ABBEY   Of the ecclesiastical buildings of the 12th century Augustinian Priory little remains except the superb west front of the Priory

Church. After the Dissolution of the Monasteries, the Priory was bought by Sir John Byron and converted into a family house, which remained in the hands of the Byrons (the fifth Sir John becoming the first Lord Byron) until 1817, when it was sold to meet the debts of the 6th Lord, the famous poet. It was presented to Nottingham City Council in 1931 and is now a Byron museum. The gardens are particularly splendid, especially the Japanese Water Garden. The Abbey grounds are open all year (admission charge at the entrance gate) and the house from Good Friday to Sept. 30th (for hours, check at the City Information Bureau). Refreshments are available. **NOTE: No public access into the Abbey from the public footpath.**

Just outside the main entrance to the Abbey grounds stands the Pilgrim Oak, said to date back to mediaeval times. By tradition, pilgrims met beneath it before passing on the the Priory.

The drive from the Lodge towards the Abbey, along which the Robin Hood Way has come, is along the line of the old main Nottingham to Mansfield road. This was known as the Great Way of the King, and in mediaeval times linked the castles of Nottingham and Bolsover. It was closed in 1760 by Act of Parliament as being dangerous! The Turnpike road from Larch Farm to Nottingham was then made.

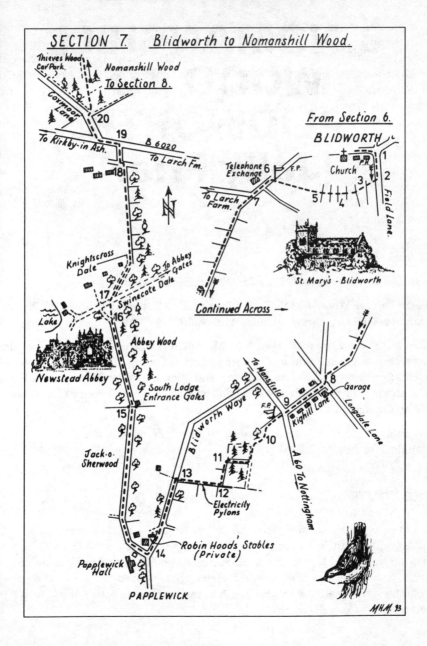

SECTION 7. Blidworth to Nomanshill Wood.

8. NOMANSHILL WOOD TO BLIDWORTH (Jolly Friar)

Distance: 8 km. (5 miles.)

Maps: Landranger Sheet 120.   1:25,000 Series Sheet SK.55.

Start: 'Thieves Wood' Car Park on minor road to Sutton-in-Ashfield off B.6020, 1 km. west of Larch Farm crossroads with A.60.

How to get there: By road, take A.60 Mansfield road from Nottingham. At the crossroads at Larch Farm, by the traffic lights at the top of a hill, turn left on to B.6020 (signposted Kirkby-in-Ashfield), and after just under 1 km., fork right on to a minor road to Sutton-in-Ashfield. The Car Park is a Forestry Commission site on the right just after a slight left-hand bend.

By public transport: For bus service to Larch Farm, enquire from the 'Bus Hotline', Tel. Nottm. 240000.

THE ROUTE

1. On entering Nomanshill Wood, do not turn right along the edge of the wood, but aim diagonally left through the wood to a belt of coniferous trees at the top of a slight incline. Continue ahead, rising and falling, ignoring left and right turns, to a T-junction with a wide forestry track beyond the trees. (If coming from the access point, cross a bridge from the car park to enter a track, turn left and continue along the route.)

NOMANSHILL WOOD TO BLIDWORTH (Jolly Friar)

Turn right along the forestry track for 200 metres.

Now turn right on another track, becoming grassy and curving left to meet a nce bordering Fountaindale School on the left. Follow this fence for 300 metres reach the A.60 by a large sign warning of disabled persons. **NOTE:** The whole the route described in this point 3 is a PERMISSIVE PATH, granted for the bin Hood Way, and not a public right-of-way. It may therefore be closed at iy time. If this should happen, retrace your steps to point 18 in Section 7. From re, where you emerge on to the B.6020, turn right for a short distance, then st left into Little Ricketts Lane. This lane leads to the A.60. Turn left along this ain road, taking care, and after about 500 metres rejoin our route at the Public idleway sign mentioned below in point 4. (If you are only walking from the cess point to Section 8, return up the minor road to the B.6020, turn left and llow B.6020 to Little Ricketts Lane, then go as above.)

On reaching the A.60 DO NOT cross the road here, but turn right along the otpath on the side of the road for 150 metres, until a Public Bridleway sign is en on the other side of the road.

Cross the road and go over a plank bridge into Harlow Wood, bearing slightly ght to a fence. (Just before leaving the road, go 50 metres right to the Sheppard one (A) in the verge to the left, then return.)

Bear left away from the fence, after 50 metres joining a wider track coming in om left, then go straight on through a wooded area for 1 km. until the track aches a crossroads of tracks.

. (See note at the end of this Section re detour to the Forest Stone (B).) ontinue straight on to the first of the Fountain Dale Lakes (C). Ignoring the ath joining from the right, continue for 200 metres to meet a path coming from ie left.

. Pass just to your right, then turn left again to resume the same direction for 00 metres, winding amongst trees.

. (See note at the end of the Section re Friar Tuck's Well (D).) At the end of the ike the path splits into two. Take the left fork, drop down and cross a small itch with the outflow of the lake on right, then continue ahead across a large pen field, keeping the stream to your right.

0. After 500 metres, turn right at a crossing of bridleways, go through trees and ver the stream into a field with a farm ahead up a rise (Providence Farm).

11. Walk straight on, keeping farm, and then hedge, to your left.

12. Go through a gate at the end of the hedge and turn right along the far drive to its junction with a road.

13. Turn left along the road and follow it for 400 metres to where it bears left.

14. Take an unmetalled lane straight ahead at the bend (New Road) for abou 1.6 km. and ignore all paths to right or left. This lane eventually become metalled and passes the Library, where the route keeps straight ahead.

15. At the T-junction with the main road (Mansfield Road), where there a toilets, turn right for approx. 100 metres.

16. Turn left by the Forest Folk Hotel, along Dale Lane and follow this road t the Jolly Friar Inn.

NOTES: At point 7 of the route an interesting detour is to turn left along a clea track for about 1.4 km., following telegraph poles and ignoring a crossing trac about two-thirds of the way along. In a field to the right, just a few metres off th track, will be seen the Forest Stone (B). To rejoin the Robin Hood Way, retrac your steps to point 7.

At point 9, where the paths divide, some 30 metres away to the right is the sit of Friar Tuck's Well (D). This is on private land, but it is hoped that at som future date it may be possible to visit it.

REFRESHMENTS

Portland Craft Centre, Mansfield Road. (slightly to left of where the Way meet A.60 at point 4) Refreshments, crafts, waymarked forest walks.

INTEREST

A. SHEPPARD STONE An inscribed stone in the grass at the side of the A.6(marks the spot where one Bessie Sheppard of Papplewick was murdered at the age of 17 in 1817.

This area was a noted haunt of highwaymen and robbers and we are reminded of this by the name of Thieves Wood.

B. FOREST STONE   This stone, which once stood in Mansfield Market Place, marked the place where the Forest Court used to meet every seven years in mediaeval times to formulate the Forest Law, and the Verderers met the Freeholders three times a year to rent pasturage. This is a similar procedure to that still in force in the New Forest. The shape of the stone suggests that it has been placed upside-down.

C. FOUNTAIN DALE LAKES   Now partly overgrown and silted, these lakes are attached to the house of that name. It was at Fountain Dale that Robin Hood first met Friar Tuck, when they fought at the moat, the remains of which are now barely discernible. Here, too, Sir Walter Scott wrote his famous novel 'Ivanhoe'. (See also notes in 'The Robin Hood Legend', at the end of this book.)

D. FRIAR TUCK'S WELL   This is an ancient well by the side of Rainworth Water. It has long been disused and has fallen into disrepair with neglect. It is now hard to find, but it is hoped that in the future it may be possible for the site to be cleared and reshaped. The Friar is said to have baptised his converts here.

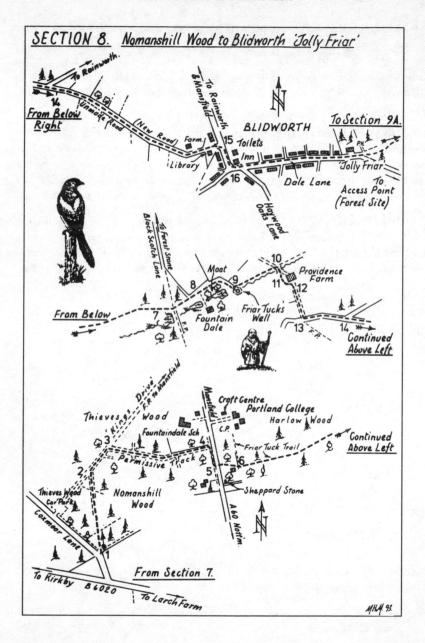

SECTION 8. Nomanshill Wood to Blidworth 'Jolly Friar'

To Rainworth.
To Rainworth & Mansfield
14 From Below Right
Unmade Road
(New Road)
BLIDWORTH
To Section 9A.
PH
Farm
15 Toilets
Inn
Jolly Friar
Library
16
Dale Lane
To Access Point (Forest Site)

Haywood Oaks Lane

To Forest Stone
Black Scotch Lane
Moat
8
9
10
11 Providence Farm
12
From Below
7
Fountain Dale
Friar Tucks Well
13
14
Continued Above Left

Kings Drive F.R. to Mansfield
Thieves Wood
Croft Centre
Portland College
Harlow Wood
3
Fountaindale Sch
4
C.P.
Friar Tuck Trail
Continued Above Left
Permissive Track
2
5
6
Sheppard Stone
Thieves Wood Car Park
Nomanshill Wood
A60 Nottm.
Coxmoor Lane
To Kirkby B6020
From Section 7.
To Larch Farm

M.H.A. 93.

9. BLIDWORTH
(Jolly Friar)
TO KIRLINGTON

FOR MAPPING PURPOSES, THIS SECTION HAS BEEN DIVIDED INTO 9a AND 9b.
SECTION 9a, BLIDWORTH TO LITTLE TURN CROFT FARM.
SECTION 9b, LITTLE TURN CROFT FARM TO KIRLINGTON.

Total distance: 23.25 km. (15.5 miles).
(9a = 17.25 km. (10.75 miles); 9b = 6 km. (3.75 miles).

Maps: Landranger Sheet 120.   1:25,000 Series Sheet SK.65.

Start: Jolly Friar Inn on Dale Lane, Blidworth.

How to get there: By road, go to the centre of Blidworth and at the Forest Folk Hotel turn along Dale Lane as far as the Jolly Friar. Some on-street parking is possible along here, and there is a Forestry Commission Car Park at Haywood Oaks, just over 500 metres further along Dale Lane towards its junction with A.614.

By public transport: For bus services to Blidworth, enquire from the 'Bus Hotline', Tel. Nottm. 240000.

THE ROUTE

Should the walker wish to break up this long section into smaller ones, convenient break points are Farnsfield and Southwell.

1. Having come along Dale Lane as far as the 'Jolly Friar', take the track which is

seen a little way beyond the Inn, with a plantation to the left.

2. At a path junction about 250 metres on, turn right with the path, the immediately left, then parallel to a hedge up to an electric sub-station seen o the left. Follow a line of telegraph poles at the hedge side.

3. At the fourth pole go straight on, cross a ditchboard and follow a ditch an hedge on right as far as a farm track.

4. Enter a large field and head across, bearing very slightly left, aiming for telegraph pole towards the far side, which carries a waymark.

5. At the far side, climb up a bank into the next field and continue across th field with a hedge to left and a high point to right.

6. At the end of this field continue in the same direction and follow th waymark posts to reach another track.

7. Cross a farm track and bear slightly left across a field to a hedge corner and waymark post.

8. Go forward with the hedge on your left to join a farm track coming in fron the right.

9. Continue on track towards Hill House Farm, seen ahead, to cross a stile i front of a barn. Veer left to a hand gate and walk forward, with a fence on th right to the A.614.

10. Cross the A.614 with care and go through a gap in the hedge by a footpatl sign, then walk straight across the field to a gap.

11. Go through this gap, then bear slightly right, aiming for a gap in the fa hedge, several metres to the right of a small building.

12. Continue in the same direction through a line of gaps across four mor fields.

13. Climb a stile and follow a hedge on your right.

14. At the end of the hedge, step to the right to enter a large field.

15. Walk in a straight line across this field to a hedge seen ahead, which you follow to reach a further stile. Go on to a grassy track between hedges ove another stile then past the Old Vicarage on your right. (At this point the mair route goes to Southwell, and then on to Kirklington. There is, however, a

.orter alternative route to Kirklington, which is described at the end of this
·ction.)

·. The track now joins a road, Vicarage Lane, at a sharp bend, by a footpath sign.
ontinue ahead and after 125 metres turn right into a ginnel which eventually
ads to a minor road.

'. Go forward through double gates to cross two fields, then bear half left to
ater a hedged track. After 200 metres veer right at a T-junction and after just over
km. turn half left across a field to enter Combs Wood, seen ahead.

·. Just inside the wood, follow the path to the right, then as you leave the trees,
alk up the hill to the right of the wood to join a hedged cart track, Robs Lane.

·. After 200 metres, at a footpath sign, the walker has the option of making a
nort detour to Robin Hood Hill, one of the finest viewpoints in Notts.

·a. If the option is taken, turn right and follow the hedge on the right to a gap, to
aeet a clear track. Turn right and after 150 metres turn left at a footpath sign to
aeet a minor road. Cross to the gate opposite, following the track until it bears
·ft, then go half right to the foot of a copse. Follow the headland path, keeping
ae trees on your left, to reach a stile. Go over this and ascend half left to the
ummit to enjoy the view. To return to the main route just retrace your steps to the
·ootpath sign on Robs Lane (Point 19).

0. Turn left along Robs Lane (turn right if coming back from Robin Hood Hill)
nd follow this sunken lane for 1.25 km., ignoring a track to the left, to reach the
oad opposite Wood Farm.

1. Turn left and after 400 metres turn right at Meadow Farm, as signed, to join a
ootpath which bears left at a waymark in front of a banked hedge, eventually
nerging into a hedged lane.

2. Proceed ahead taking the first lane on the right to pass in front of Little Turn
:roft Farm.

·ROM HERE, THE ROUTE IS NOW SHOWN ON THE MAPS AS SECTION 9b.

·ollow this track to a T-junction then go forward on to a headland path which
·ventually descends to a footbridge. Continue past a tennis court on the right to
oin the access drive of Manor Farm, which leads on to a road, Beck Lane, Halam.

3. Turn right and after a double bend take the hedged path on the left and come

out into a field. Bear half right up the hill to a stile seen on the skyline in so
trees. Proceed in the same direction to pass to the right of a house, to a road.

24. Turn right, then go straight ahead at a crossroads. After 300 metres, whe
the road bends left, keep straight ahead to a stile on the left. Cross the field t
minor road.

25. Turn right and after a double bend, go left at a footpath sign., Follow t
headland path until the hedge turns left, then turn right, up the hill, to a hed
on the left. At the bottom of a second field turn right at a path junction, and aft
75 metres turn left up the headlands of two fields to meet another county road.

26. Turn left and continue, eventually to meet the A.612 Nottingham to Sout
well road. Here turn right up the road, then take the first lane left, in front
Brackenhurst Agricultural College. After 500 metres take the left-hand road a
junction.

27. After 300 metres take the footpath to the right, by the side of kenne
passing alongside Home Farm, to emerge on to another lane. Go forward for 1
metres, then take the well-defined path, left, at the bend in the road. C
reaching the corner of two hedges, bear half right to follow a clear headla
which turns left and descends to a narrow path between wire fences.

28. At the bottom, turn right and after a few metres, left over a footbridge
pass up the right-hand side of the Recreation Ground. Turn right at the Mer
orial Gates, then forward past the Bishop's Palace ruins on the right, to reac
Southwell Minster. (A).

**For walkers wishing to join the route at Southwell, the Car Park is on Chur
Street, across the road from the Minster.**

29. Leave the grounds of Southwell Minster by the north gate, leading on
Church Street, and turn right for 150 metres to a ginnel on the left, just past th
house called Normanton Prebend. After a few metres cross to a stile into a fiel
and walk forward parallel to a wall and hedge on right, to a waymarked stile.

30. Go over this stile, cross a road (Shady Lane) and take the stile and step
opposite to enter a second field. Continue ahead, bearing left to the far corne
and a tall hedge, to meet a narrow path alongside a stream, the Potwell Dyk
which eventually emerges on to Kirklington Road.

31. Cross over to the tarmac path and on to an estate road, which bears righ then at the end take a ginnel, which leads to Newark Road.

32. At the road turn left, then left again after 15 metres, to join the clear path which follows the River Greet. After 300 metres climb some steps and turn right to come on to Station Road.

33. Turn right along the road, and just past Caudwell's Mill and the River Greet, turn left at a signpost.

34. The path now follows the River Greet for 2 km. before turning left over a footbridge to pass in front of Maythorne Mill.

35. Follow the access road to meet the Southwell Trail (B), a former railway line.

36. Turn right along the Trail for 2.5 km., until you reach the buildings of the old Kirklington Station, now a private house. There is a public Car Park and Picnic Site here.

THE SHORTER ALTERNATIVE ROUTE FROM FARNSFIELD TO KIRKLINGTON IS AS FOLLOWS:

15a. Where the track meets Vicarage Lane at a sharp bend by a footpath sign, turn left over a stile and cross a field towards a white cottage and a bus shelter on the main road through the village of Farnsfield (C).

15b. Climb the fence and cross the road, then take the signposted footpath up the steps to the left of the white cottage, up a bank on to a recreation ground.

15c. Cross the recreation ground diagonally to the right, to a footpath sign in the far corner, leading to a road.

15d. Turn left along this road until you see a road junction about 100 metres ahead of you, then turn right through a wide gateway, which is the drive into the former Farnsfield Station, now a picnic site at the start of the Southwell Trail (B). See the large sign as you enter this drive.

15e. Pass the old shunting yard and outbuildings to reach the start of the Trail. Turn right along the disused railway and follow it for about 2.5 km. to the Car Park and Picnic Site at the former Kirklington Station.

REFRESHMENTS

White Post, Farnsfield (on main road A.614)   Restaurant, Bar Meals.

Red Lion, Farnsfield   Bar meals.

Wagon & Horses, Halam   Bar meals.

The Bramley Apple, Southwell   Bar meals.

Newcastle Arms, Southwell   Bar meals.

INTEREST

A. SOUTHWELL MINSTER The jewel in the crown of Southwell is undoubtedly the exquisite Minster, one of our smallest cathedrals, yet one of the most architecturally exciting. The present building is Norman, with many fine arches, mouldings and other features, but the site was in use before the Normans came, and there are some Roman remains inside the building. There is not enough room in this Guide to do justice to this superb building, but there are several other books which go into more detail, which are on sale in the Minster bookshop.

Southwell itself is a fine example of a large rural community and is famous for several old buildings, including the Saracen's Head, an old coaching inn; the ruins of the Bishop's Palace; Burgage Manor, which the poet Lord Byron visited during vacations from Cambridge; and the Prebends. These were the houses where the Prebendaries (or Canons) lived, and are named after the villages where their estate and parish lay. The College of Prebendaries has long been abolished and no Prebendaries live in these houses, though their names have been preserved. Southwell is also the place where the original Bramley apple was discovered by chance, and a pub is named after it. Southwell makes an ideal place to take a day off from walking the Robin Hood Way, being almost exactly at the halfway point of the route. It is full of beauty and historical associations and is highly recommended as a worthwhile 'diversion'. There are numerous eating-places, and overnight accommodation is available.

B. SOUTHWELL TRAIL This part of the former Southwell–Mansfield railway line was purchased by Notts. County Council and has been turned into a trail for walkers, cyclists and horse-riders. Though without steep gradients, as befits a ailway line, it has some very attractive stretches in cuttings, and gives a good anorama of this part of Eastern Notts.

2. **FARNSFIELD** An attractive red-brick village with refreshment facilities and shops. Nearby are two ancient Camps, one at Combs Farm, 2 km. S.W., and the other at Hexgreave Park. The tiny building to the left of the steps to the Recreation Ground, which our short-cut route passes, is the former village lock-up'.

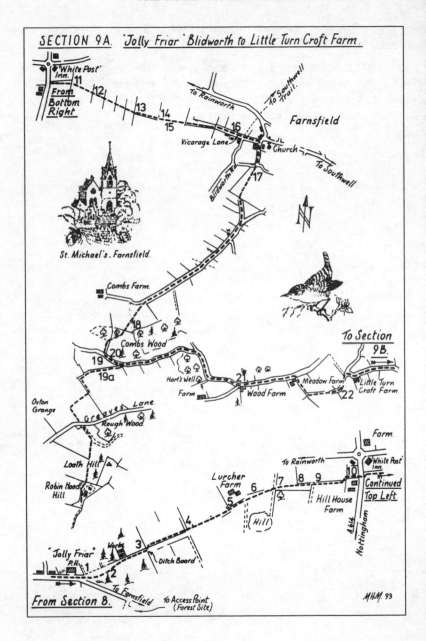

SECTION 9A. 'Jolly Friar' Blidworth to Little Turn Croft Farm.

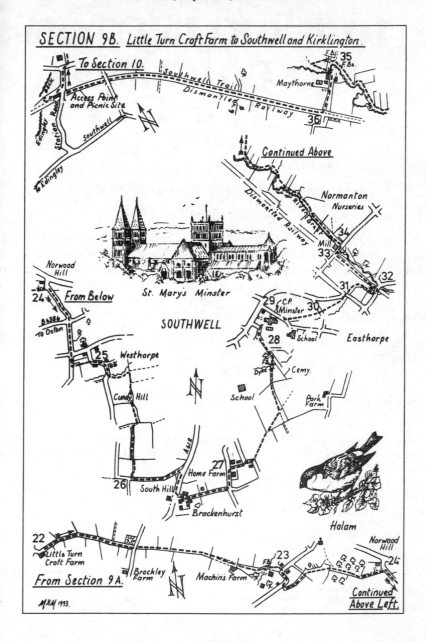

SECTION 9B. *Little Turn Croft Farm to Southwell and Kirklington.*

To Section 10.

Southwell Trail

Dismantled Railway

Access Point and Picnic Site

Southwell

To Edingley

Maythorne

35

36

Continued Above

Normanton Nurseries

Dismantled Railway

34

Mill

33

31

32

St. Mary's Minster

Norwood Hill

24

From Below

B6386

To Oxton

25

Westhorpe

Cundy Hill

29

C.P. Minster

30

28

School

Eastthorpe

Dyke

Cemy.

School

Park Farm

SOUTHWELL

A612

27

Home Farm

26

South Hill

Brackenhurst

Halam

Norwood Hill

22

Little Turn Croft Farm

From Section 9A.

Brockley Farm

Machins Farm

FB

23

24

Continued Above Left.

M.H.M 1993.

10. KIRKLINGTON TO EAKRING

Distance: 8.5 km. (5.3 miles)

Maps: Landranger Sheet 120.   1:25,000 Series Sheet SK.65. and SK.66.

Start: Kirklington Station Picnic Place on Southwell Trail.

How to get there: Join A.617, Mansfield to Newark road and at Kirklington village leave this road by a minor road into the village, just west of the church. After 1 km. along this road, take the road on the right signposted to Car Park. The Car Park is just off this road to the right by a track passing the building of the former railway station. The Car Park can also be reached by minor road from Southwell and Farnsfield.

By public transport: For local bus services, phone the 'Bus Hotline' on Nottm 240000.

THE ROUTE

1. At Kirklington Station leave the Southwell Trail and rise along the entrance track past the old Station House to reach the minor road at the Car Park entrance sign.

2. Turn left for 150 metres to a T-junction, then turn right for a few metres to footpath sign to Kirklington.

3. Turn left at this sign and follow hedge, then fence, to a footbridge over a dyke on your left.

4. Turn left over the footbridge with a pond on your right, to another footbridge over a second dyke.

. On the far side of this footbridge turn left along dyke, then bear right at a hedge junction, heading straight towards Kirklington Church.

. Shortly there is a kissing gate in the hedge to your left. Go through it, then resume previous direction.

'. At the far side of the field, by the end of the garden of a large new house, go ight, through a kissing gate, and head towards a garage.

. Turn left along driveway, on to a tarmac road into Kirklington (A), passing he Post Office on right and church on left.

. At junction with main road (A.617) turn right for about 300 metres.

10. Just before a left-hand bend in the road, and in sight of a by-road to Normanton, cross main road and enter farm track to a gate which is the entrance o Hall Farm. Continue about 20 metres beyond gate to the first farm building on eft.

11. Go right into a field, using the left-hand of two gateways, and follow track curving left past trees.

12. Go through another gateway and follow clear track uphill. The lake and grounds of Rodney School are now down to your left.

13. At the top of the hill the track bears right through a double gateway and continues clearly towards a distant group of barns. Avoid a track going left.

14. On reaching barns keep to the right of them, bearing left to the corner of a wood, where bear right alongside a dyke on your right.

15. At the far end of this field the path meets an overgrown green lane known as Whitestub Lane. Turn right along this ancient track, winding through the trees, to a junction of dykes.

16. Cross a plank bridge on your left and keep to the right-hand edge of the field, along the outer edge of Roe Wood (B).

17. Near the end of this wood cross over a small dyke with waymarks. Now bear right, still along outside of the wood.

18. Where the wood goes sharp right, turn left across a small field to cross a culverted dyke. Continue into next field, taking a line towards the farm (Holywell Farm).

19. When in line with farm boundary fence aim left towards stile seen in th corner.

20. Go over stile into a paddock, then cross three further stiles to reach an ope field.

21. Cross the first field on a field edge path with field boundary on right. The cross two further fields to reach Orchard Wood Farm. Pass this farm on its rig side, onto the farm track. Walk to an electric power post to rear of farm, the turn left and cross field towards end of hedge and tree, seen ahead. Go over ditchboard into the next field. Continue along the field edge, downhill, to a dyl crossed by a cart bridge.

22. Continue across the next field straight ahead, aiming for a gap into th wood, and cross a plank bridge into Dilliner Wood (C).

23. Keep straight ahead through the wood on a clear muddy track and pas through a hedge gap into an expanse of wild uncultivated common land Mansey Common (D).

24. The Way is now not very clear, but in fact bears left (NNW direction) fc about 450 metres to a footpath sign on a post.

25. Turn right at this post and follow a clearer path, winding through scrub an waymarked at intervals, until you reach a footbridge.

26. Cross footbridge and climb the bank on the far side. At the top of the ban go left for a few metres with hedge on left, then strike to the right, across th field, keeping parallel to power lines about 45 metres to your left, and descend t a crossing farm track.

27. At the farm track go left for a very few metres, then right, over a plan bridge, then slightly left towards a gap in the far hedge.

28. At this gap cross a cart bridge and continue ahead up a rise to the corner of hedge.

29. At the corner, go over a stile to left of hedge and take a path with hedge o right. At the end of the field go through gap, then go right for a few metres, t reach a grassy track and then bear slightly left to the road through Eakring (E).

30. Turn right along the road for a short distance, then left up Side Lane.

31. Where Side Lane turns right and becomes Back Lane, keep straight ahea

ong a narrow path between hedges and over a stile, then follow the hedge on
our right as far as another hedge. Turn right for a few metres, then left along a
edge side (hedge on your right), heading for a group of trees, and reach a stile
ading on to a gravel farm track.

2. Cross this track and, slightly to your left, find a plank bridge leading up a
mall hillock to Pulpit Ash (F). Visit this then return to the gravel track and turn
ft, slightly downhill, towards a farm.

3. At a T-junction turn right along another track which soon turns left, then
ecomes a grassy track as far as farm buildings on left.

4. At the farm buildings a minor road comes from the right. Continue straight
head to a road junction at the sign 'Church Lane' and turn left to reach the
avile Arms Inn on a corner.

REFRESHMENTS

Only one, at the end!
avile Arms, Eakring   Bar snacks.

INTEREST

A. KIRKLINGTON   This village, situated just above the little River Greet, has
a church with old stones and interesting human heads among the carvings.
Kirklington Hall, 18th century, now houses the Rodney School.

B. ROE WOOD   This wood is a Site of Special Scientific Interest.

C. DILLINER WOOD   Another interesting wood, unusual in being almost
entirely of hardwoods.

D. MANSEY COMMON   This is the only remaining one of the three Com-
mons which used to exist in the parish of Eakring, the others being Enclosed
Common and Penny Pastures. Though now obviously out of use as common
grazing land, it is a very interesting piece of wild country which is reverting to
woodland by natural colonisation. It is rich in insect, bird, animal and plant life,
and of great scientific interest, as well as being perhaps the wildest and most
natural piece of countryside in Notts. Its future is at present in dispute, but it is

one of the sites in the County most worth preserving.

E. EAKRING   An interesting village with fine red-roofed houses, somewha
withdrawn from the busy life of the County, Eakring was one of the few fre
manors in the district not owned by the monks of Rufford. Farming was of th
'open field' type and all the lanes to the village were gated. A number of then
still remain as 'green lanes'. The village once boasted 7 pubs, of which only on
remains. Eakring's principal place in history is that in 1670 a new vicar wa
appointed. He was the Rev. William Mompesson, the heroic Rector of Eyam, th
Derbyshire village whose population was decimated by the Great Plague o
1665. The villagers of Eakring, however, feared that he had brought the infectio
with him, and refused to allow him into the village. He was compelled to live i
a rude shelter in Rufford Park and to hold his services under an ash tree in
large field in the parish. In the 20th century Eakring has earned itself anothe
entry in the history books, for it was here in 1939 that oil was discovered, an
Eakring became the largest on-shore oilfield in Britain. The oil supplies are
unfortunately, pretty well exhausted now, though the odd well still operates i
some of the surrounding villages. A few sites of derelict wells can still be seen i
the woods close to some of the local footpaths.

F. PULPIT ASH   On this site stood the ash tree under which the Rev. Willian
Mompesson used to hold his services. The original tree was destroyed b
lightning, but a young tree has been planted in its place, and a memorial cros
and stone erected on the site.

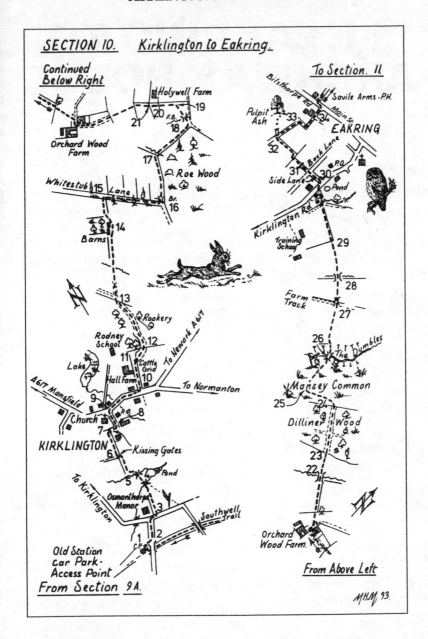

11. EAKRING TO ARCHWAY HOUSE

Distance: 10 km. (6.25 miles.)

Maps: Landranger Sheet 120.   1:25,000 Series Sheet SK.66.

Start: Eakring village. Park carefully on side lanes.

How to get there: By road: turn off A.614 (Nottingham to Ollerton road) approx. 6 km. south of the Ollerton island, on a road signposted Eakring. The village is about 3.5 km. along this road.

By public transport: For local bus services, enquire from the 'Bus Hotline' Tel. Nottm. 240000.

THE ROUTE

1. At the 'Savile Arms' turn right on Wellow Road and walk to just beyond the old windmill, where there is a stile on the left-hand side, by an old gate.

2. Go over the stile and head towards another stile on the far side of the field, then bear slightly right to a wide gap in the far hedge.

3. Go through the gap: and across a farm track, then cross the next large field, aiming just left of the spinney on the hilltop.
N.B. Diversions are planned at points 2 & 3 and will be waymarked when they have been agreed. The diversions will be as follows:

(2a. Go over the stile, turn right and follow the field edge path, making several turns, to reach a farm track.

3a. Turn right along this track and follow the field edge as far as the Spinney. Turn left along outside edge of the spinney to reach the hedge which goes

60

leftwards down hill. It is hoped that the spinney will eventually bear some sort of commemoration of the Robin Hood Way.)

4. At crest of the hill look slightly left for a stile in the hedge which goes down the hill. Go over this double stile and continue towards a field gate lower down and slightly to the right.

5. The gate leads to a bridge over a disused railway, which is crossed. Then continue ahead across a field, through a crossing line of trees, to a wooden electricity pylon.

6. By the pylon cross a ditchboard and continue straight across the next field, aiming for the right-hand edge of the large poultry-farm building in the distance, to meet a card track..

6. By the pylon cross a ditchboard and continue straight across the next field, aiming for the right-hand edge of the large poultry-farm buildings in the distance, to meet a cart track.

7. Turn right on the cart track and follow it to a T-junction, passing a farm cottage on the right.

7a. At this T-junction it is worth while turning right and walking for a few metres to North Laiths Farm. At the far end of the farm buildings is an interesting dovecote, where doves can still be seen. Then return.

8. At the T-junction turn left along a clear track, which is metalled at first, then rough. On approaching a plantation, do not go towards it, but bear left, to pass a house and stables.

9. The track, now metalled again, is joined by another one coming from the right. Keep in the same direction towards another plantation, to reach another T-junction.

10. Turn left, then cross a bridge over a stream. (This is Rainworth Water, which flows out of Rufford Lake). It is hoped that in the near future a new access will be made into Rufford Park at the corner by this bridge, which will then be incorporated in our route.

11. Follow the stream for a short distance to a junction of tracks, then turn left at a waymark, heading for a bungalow.

12. After about 300 metres, just after the bungalow on the left, turn right by a row of poplars, along a rough track into a small plantation.

13. Ignore a left turn and follow outside edge of the plantation, towards farm buildings, and at these buildings pass to their left, going slightly down hill through trees to emerge on to A.614.

13a. At this point a worth-while detour is to turn right along A.614 and walk to the entrance to Rufford Park (A), and then into the Park, where there are refreshments, toilets, shops and car parking. There is a very fine walk around the Park (see Notes). Having visited the Park, return to the entrance and walk back along A.614 to return to our route.

14. Cross the A.614 with care and go along the metalled road opposite. Where this turns left into the Holiday Village keep straight ahead on an unmade track and after 200 metres turn right at the waymark.

15. Follow the hedge line on your right to a small plantation.

16. Turn left along outside of plantation for about 100 metres to a gap leading into the plantation.

17. Follow a narrow path from the gap through the plantation, to come to the end of a hedge, and follow this with the hedge on your right, across a large field to a road (B.6030).

18. Cross the road but DO NOT take the footpath opposite. Instead, turn left along the road for 200 metres to the entrance to Holly Farm.

19. Turn right along the driveway and pass the farm buildings to their left. Enter a large field to join a hedgeline, which is followed downhill across fields to another road.

20. Cross this road, go through the gate opposite and cross the field with hedge on left, to a railway line. Cross this line and maintain the same direction to reach the bank of the River Maun.

21. At the junction with the path along the river bank, turn left and follow the river. The path then bears right to cross two bridges and reach a T-junction with a path which comes from Edwinstowe.

22. Turn left and follow the clear track along a long narrow field with hedge on right for 500 metres, then continue between fences, close to the river on the left, and reach a wide gap in a crossing hedge.

22a. At this point it is possible to turn left and follow a wide track under railway bridges to the Dog and Duck Inn, near which are the remains of King John's Palace (B).

23. At the gap, turn right up a wide track towards Archway House (C).

24. Pass to the left of Archway House along a wide earth track and follow this as it winds through a plantation to meet a road (A.6075).

REFRESHMENTS

Savile Arms, Eakring Bar snacks.

'Coachhouse' and 'Buttery' Restaurants, Rufford Park Meals, snacks, drinks.

INTEREST

A. RUFFORD ABBEY AND PARK The Cistercian Abbey was founded in 1148 by Gilbert de Gaunt, Earl of Lincoln, and at the Dissolution the Estate was granted to the Earl of Shrewsbury. The present house, first built in Elizabethen times, was allowed to fall into decay, but is being restored. The stables now contain cafes, a shop and gallery and the Administration Office, as well as toilets, and there is a large Car Park. The surrounding 130-acre Park, too, was sadly neglected, the Lake in particular becoming badly silted up and empty, partly because of mining subsidence. It has now been dredged, drained and refilled, and is a wildfowl reserve. Attractive walks have been created all around the Lake and the whole Park opened to the public. A former formal garden has been restored below the Orangery, and other places worth visiting are the ancient Ice House in the woods – a kind of early refrigerator where meat was kept under cold conditions – and the restored Mill at the Wellow end of the Park, which has a landing stage and a car park. Leaflets about Rufford, published by Notts. County Council, are obtainable at the Abbey.

B. KING JOHN'S PALACE A little way off our route, behind the Dog and Duck Inn in the village of Old Clipstone, lie the scanty remains of King John's Palace, believed to have been built by Edwin, the first Christian King of Northumbria. It was visited by Henry II, Richard the Lionheart and William the Lion of Scotland, and was used as a hunting lodge, and had a park in the time of

Henry II. The Palace started to decay in the time of Henry IV and the few remains are now a preserved monument. It is said that Robin Hood attacked the palace from his quarters at Creswell Crags and released some hostages.

C. ARCHWAY HOUSE   This building, also known as the Duke's Folly, was built by the Duke of Portland in 1842 as a copy of the Gatehouse to Worksop Priory. The facade has a number of interesting sculptures, including statues of Robin Hood and several of his associates. Similar statues are found at Bestwood Lodge on the outskirts of Nottingham (see Section 5 of this Guide). The walls are buttressed and there are traceried windows on both sides of the central arch. The house was once used as a school and is still a (private) residence. The turf 'ride' running through the Archway was intended to enable the Duke to drive from Welbeck to Nottingham.

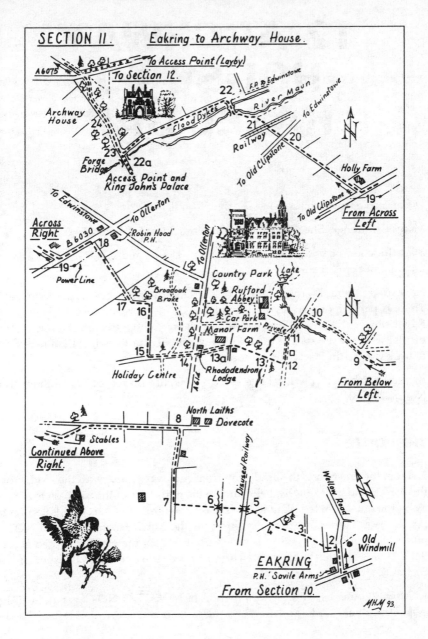

12. ARCHWAY HOUSE TO HAZEL GAP

Distance: 6.5 km. (4 miles.)

Maps: Landranger Sheet 120.   1:25,000 Series Sheet SK.66, SK.56 & SK. 57.

Start: Junction of bridleway from Archway House and A.6075, 2 km. west of Edwinstowe crossroads.

How to get there: By road, take A.6075 from Edwinstowe towards Mansfield. There is parking in a lay-by on the north side of the road, about 1.5 km. from Edwinstowe, also limited parking in a small area within the forest a few metres further west, by the start of the bridleway past Centre Tree. It is then necessary to walk west to the start of this section.

By public transport: For local bus services, enquire from the 'Bus Hotline', Tel. Nottm. 240000.

THE ROUTE

1. From the junction of the bridleway from Archway House with the road, cross the A.6075 and go through a field gate on the north side of the road, on to a track along the outside of the plantation. (**Please note:** from the start of this section to point 5 is a 'permissive path', granted for the Robin Hood Way, and NOT a public right-of-way, though it is much used. It may therefore be closed at any time. If this should happen, an alternative route is given at the end of the Section.)

2. After 300 metres, at a 3-way junction of tracks, DO NOT bear right. (The major track here leads to the site of the famous tree known as Robin Hood's larder, which has now disappeared.) Instead bear left, still on the outside edge of the plantation, to meet a hedge, which is then followed for another 300 metres.

3. Opposite a forestry track going right, into the forest, step left for about 5 metres to the site of St. Edwin's Chapel (A), then return and continue in the original direction.

4. Ignore the next track going right, cross a second track and pass through a gateway and across a narrow stretch of plantation to a T-junction with a clear bridleway by a yellow water hydrant marker.

5. Turn right along the bridleway. After about 400 metres a forestry track comes up from the left. Keep straight ahead, now on this track.

6. After about 1 km. the forestry track bears right to a narrow metalled road, which should be followed.

7. After about 530 metres a gravel track crosses the road. Turn left on this track, rising slightly into trees.

8. About 60 metres on, the gravel track swings left, but the route keeps straight ahead along a narrower path.

9. After some 60 metres the trees on the right finish. Turn right at this point, along a grassy track between the plantation and a hedge, rising at first, then descending between hedges. Go over a stile by the side of a crossing gate and continue ahead to the buildings of Gleadthorpe Grange and a road.

10. Cross the road and go up a metalled track with farm buildings on right, pass through a metal gate and continue to a 'crossroads' of tracks.

11. DO NOT take the obvious track straight ahead which is not a right-of-way, but turn right along an earth track, which soon runs between barbed wire fences, then enters a plantation. Follow this track, which later runs along the outside of another plantation, to pass through a gateway on to the A.616 at Hazel Gap.

11a. To reach the nearest large car park, which is the Access Point for the next Section, turn right and walk along the road for 1.5 km. to the Forestry Commission Picnic Site at Fanny's Grove.

The route of the Robin Hood Way continues straight across the A.616.

NOTE: If the 'permissive path' at the start of this Section is closed, on reaching the A.6075 from Archway House, turn left and walk along the road for nearly 2 km. to a crossroads (junction of A.6075 and B.6035 to Warsop). On the right at this crossroads, leading off the A.6075, will be found the start of the bridleway which is joined at point 5. The bridleway should be followed as far as the yellow water hydrant marker mentioned in para 4, then the described route can be resumed.

REFRESHMENTS

Sorry, this Section is DRY! The nearest are in Edwinstowe, near the start.

INTEREST

A. ST. EDWIN'S CHAPEL   A pile of stones surmounted by a cross, and with an inscribed stone, marks the site of a Chantry Chapel dedicated to St. Edwin (King Edwin of Northumbria). The Chantry was banned by Henry VIII.

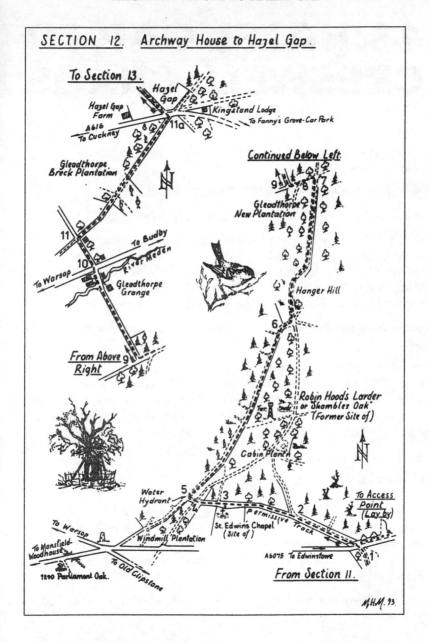

SECTION 12. Archway House to Hazel Gap.

To Section 13.

Hazel Gap

Hazel Gap Farm
A616
To Cuckney

Kingsland Lodge
To Fanny's Grove-Car Park

11a

Continued Below Left.

Gleadthorpe Breck Plantation

Gleadthorpe New Plantation

9 8 7

11

To Budby

To Warsop 10 River Meden

Gleadthorpe Grange

Hanger Hill

6

From Above Right 9

Robin Hood's Larder or Shambles Oak (Former Site of)

Cabin Plantn

Water Hydrant 5 3

To Access Point (Lay by)

St. Edwins Chapel (Site of)

Permissive Track

2

To Warsop

To Mansfield-Woodhouse

Windmill Plantation

To Old Clipstone

A6075 To Edwinstowe

From Section 11.

1290 Parliament Oak.

M.H.M. 93.

13. HAZEL GAP TO CRESWELL CRAGS

Distance: 9.5 km. (5.9 miles)

Maps: Landranger Sheet 120.   1:25,000 Series Sheet SK.56 & SK.57.

Start: Hazel Gap, on A.616 about 4 km. east of Cuckney village.

How to get there: By road, take A.616 (Ollerton to Sheffield) and park at the Forestry Commission Car Park and Picnic Site at Fanny's Grove, about 400 metres N.W. of the triangular junction between A.616, B.6005 and a minor road to Meden Vale. Then walk about 1.5 km. north-west along A.616 to Hazel Gap (there is at present no footpath link between Fanny's Grove and Hazel Gap).

By public transport: For bus services, enquire from the 'But Hotline', Te. Nottm. 240000.

From point 1 to 7 of this Section the route crosses private land which belongs to Welbeck Estates Ltd., areas of which are used for breeding game and are subject to letting for the purposes of shooting. Other parts are used for managed farming and forestry. It is essential that walkers remain strictly on the described route, all of which is on footpaths, bridleways and country roads.

THE ROUTE

1. From the north side of the A.616, facing north, DO NOT take either of the two signposted tracks to the right, but take the left-hand track. This is an old County road, now unmaintained. Follow it as it curves left through plantations to pass a house, Corunna Lodge (A) and meet a minor road. You are now in Welbeck Park (B).

2. Turn left along this minor road and pass another Lodge, Bentinck Lodge (C) on your left.

. Continue along the road to where it bends left at a barrier with a 'Strictly 'rivate' notice; bear left with the road and continue into Norton village, going ound a sharp left-hand bend opposite a telephone kiosk.

. Shortly after the left-hand bend take the road turning right, signposted Iolbeck and Worksop, and continue along it, climbing slightly to pass the 'illage name-sign.

. About 100 metres beyond the name-sign go right, over a stile and follow the 1edgeline on your left, across a long narrow field, to a kissing-gate leading onto a road opposite yet another Lodge, Bunkers Hill Lodge (D).

ia. At point 5 it is possible to make a diversion for refreshments at the Green-dale Oak Inn (E) in Cuckney village, by turning left off the road (instead of right) and following a waymarked footpath. It will then be necessary to return to point 5.

. At the Lodge bear left along the road, through a handgate, and follow a beautiful tree-lined drive with attractive views, passing Park Lodge on the right after 600 metres and then entering Tile Kiln Wood. Continue to a barrier, then bear right along the main drive, ignoring a minor road from the left.

7. Turn left at the next barrier, along a minor road, to Main Gates Lodge and a major road, A.60.

8. Cross A.60 and head towards Holbeck Woodhouse. Ignore the first right turn.

9. Take the second right turn, signposted 'Footpath Only', along a lovely avenue of evenly-spaced lime trees. This passes St. Winifred's Chapel (F) on your left, then meets a road in Holbeck village, opposite Hillside Cottage.

10. Turn left, then immediate right on a signposted footpath to Creswell Crags. This runs between hedges to a stile, then with the hedge on the left for 2 fields.

11. At the third field, keep ahead between a row of widely-spaced trees on the right and a hedge on the left, to a stile into a 4th field. Cross this field with hedge on right and the 5th field similarly.

12. On entering the 6th field, continue uphill following a line midway between two woods. At the top of a hill, aim for a stile at the right-hand corner of the field. Cross this stile and continue following a stone wall to the brow of the hill.

13. At the brow of the hill, where the wall turns right, go slightly to the left to drop down the slope into the valley of Creswell Crags (G), bearing right to cross a stile at a stone wall and coming to the edge of a stream.

14. On reaching the stream, turn right and continue, keeping the stream to your left, to the far end of a small lake, and a T-junction of paths.

15. Turn left and proceed to the edge of the road, then turn sharp right and go down a path through a small wood to reach the Visitor Centre (H).

REFRESHMENTS

Greendale Oak, Cuckney   Bar meals, snacks.

Creswell Crags Visitor Centre   Snacks, refreshments.

INTEREST

A. CORUNNA LODGE   Named after a battle in the Peninsular War, this is one of several fine Lodge Houses built by the Dukes of Portland for estate workers, which are especially to be found in Welbeck Park.

B. WELBECK PARK   A beautiful Park surrounding Welbeck Abbey. Unfortunately, except for a few minor roads and two or three footpaths (which we use on our rote), there is no public access. Welbeck Abbey was founded in 1153 by the white canons of the Premonstratensian Order under Thomas de Cuckney. They had free liberty to kill venison or any game. After the Dissolution, the estate eventually came into the possession of the Dukes of Portland, who transformed it into a magnificent house. The Abbey is now an Army boarding school, Welbeck College, and is, therefore, STRICTLY PRIVATE.

C. BENTINCK LODGE   One of the fine Lodges mentioned above. Across the road from this Lodge is a memorial to Lord George Bentinck, brother of the 5th Duke of Portland, who died near here whilst walking. He was the M.P. for Kings Lynn and a distinguished politician who was at one time regarded as a potential Prime Minister.

D. BUNKERS HILL LODGE   This Lodge is distinctive for the magnificent wrought-iron gates at its side.

E. GREENDALE OAK INN This Inn is named after the Greendale Oak, a tree which became famous because of its size. The first Duke of Portland said that he could drive a carriage through it, and to prove it, had an arch cut out of the trunk, measuring 10 feet 3 inches in height and 6 feet 3 inches across the centre. The oak has now gone, but the timber removed from the tree was made into a cabinet.

F. ST. WINIFRED'S CHURCH, HOLBECK WOODHOUSE This small church, by Louis Ambler, 1913, was erected entirely by labour on the estate, by the instructions of the Duke & Duchess of Portland. The church creates a shrine to the Portland family, with the windows at the west end, rich and luminous in colour, like jewels in a sombre setting, having the gracious Duchess depicted as Saint Winifred: The graveyard is immaculate, with tombs of many of the family to be found here, some having been exhumed from the burial ground near Welbeck Abbey.

G. CRESWELL CRAGS This lovely limestone gorge, through which the Notts./Derbys. border runs, is one of the oldest known inhabited places in Britain. There are numerous caves on both sides of the little valley, in which the remains of many prehistoric animals have been found, also the earliest known remains of modern man in Britain, after whom a whole culture has been named – the Creswellian Culture, dating back 13000 years. The caves were also inhabited by Neanderthal Man some 60000 years ago. As recently as 1978 a rockfall uncovered new remains dating back 8500 years, including artefacts and numerous bones, among them an almost complete skull of a wolf. The area was frequented by Robin Hood, and one of the caves bears his name. For further information, consult the Visitor Centre.

H. CRESWELL CRAGS VISITOR CENTRE A newly-developed centre initiated jointly by Notts. County Council and Derbys. County Council as an information centre. Books, slides, etc. about the Crags can be bought here, and lectures and film shows are often arranged. From the Centre at summer weekends there are frequent guided walks to the area of the caves, as well as other guided walks. A leaflet and News Letter on these activities will be sent free to anyone who leaves their name and address at the Centre, or writes to The Ranger, Creswell Crags Visitor Centre, Crags Road, Creswell, Worksop, Notts.

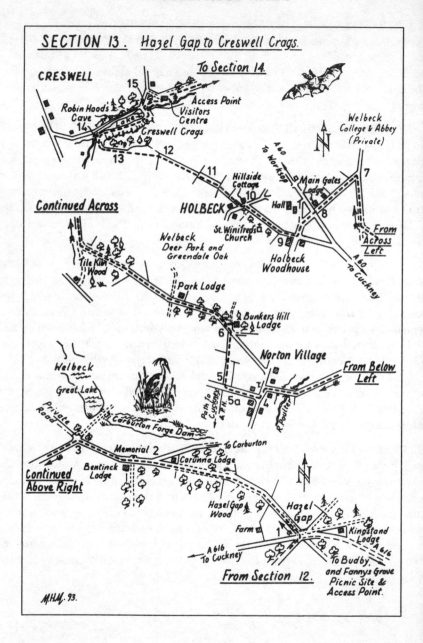

SECTION 13. Hazel Gap to Creswell Crags.

14. CRESWELL CRAGS TO CLUMBER PARK

Distance: 10.25 km. (6.4 miles.)

Maps: Landranger Sheet 120.   1:25,000 Series Sheet SK.57 & SK.67.

Start: Creswell Crags Visitor Centre Car Park.

How to get there: By road – from A.60 Mansfield to Worksop road turn on to B.6042 about halfway between Worksop and Cuckney; or from A.616 Ollerton to Sheffield road, turn on to B.6042 just on the south-east side of Creswell village. The Visitor Centre is about halfway along B.6042 and is signposted.

By public transport – for bus services, enquire from the 'Bus Hotline', Tel. Nottm. 240000.

THE ROUTE

From point 2 to point 8 the route crosses private land which belongs to Welbeck Estates Ltd., areas of which are used for breeding purposes for game-birds and are subject to letting for the purpose of shooting. Other parts are used for managed farming and forestry. It is essential that walkers remain strictly on the described route, all of which is on footpaths, bridleways and county roads.

1. After seeing the Visitor Centre, rejoin the wide track leading away from the road and past the Car Park, through woods, to meet the main road A.60.

2. Cross A.60 and take the metalled road opposite, with a bridleway sign. This road is lined with conifers.

75

3. At a Y-junction near a Lodge, go half left along a concrete road going slightl' uphill. At the top of the rise bear right and head towards a plantation, taking n' side turnings. The large building to the right was the Duke's Riding School (A).

4. Just before reaching the plantation, cross a cattle grid and turn left along a grassy track with a fence on left. Go through a gate and continue around the outside of the plantation, then descend to a hand-gate in the corner of the field. The roofs now visible to the right are those of Welbeck Abbey (B).

5. Go through the gate, bear right and continue to join a tarmac track. Turn righ' and go for a few metres to a junction, turn left and, after 100 metres, left again' over the end of the Great Lake of Welbeck.

6. Across the next field is a line of rough land. This marks the line of the' Welbeck Tunnel (C). Walk parallel to this and just to the right of it. The line o' the tunnel is marked by circular depressions in the ground, which are skylight' to light and ventilate the tunnel. Most of them are capped with concrete, bu' some are not, so whilst it is possible to go right to them, care should be taken Having followed this line right across the field, you come into sight of a battlemented Lodge, South Lodge. Just round the back of this Lodge is the entrance to the tunnel, but this is boarded up and not very inspiring.

7. As you approach the Lodge, at the edge of the small plantation on the left is a bridleway sign. Go through a handgate into the plantation, then turn right along the side of a wooden fence to another handgate with a green bridleway sign. Turn left past an iron gateway towards the Lodge. When you almost reach the Lodge buildings, DO NOT turn left on to the signposted footpath to Worksop, but turn right into trees, going towards an iron fence running away to the right.

8. On the clear track (Drinking Pit Lane) go towards the right, keeping the iron fence on your right, through a low sandstone gorge (note the carved graffiti) and continue along the track, ignoring all side turns, for about 3 km., passing two Lodges on the way. The track then meets a road, B.6005, at Sod Banks.

9. Cross the road, go through a gate and enter another clear track, which shortly meets a tarmac road. Go to the right on this road to an imposing Lodge, Truman's Lodge. Note the arched gateway.

10. DO NOT go through the arch, but continue along the road, bearing left in front of the Lodge.

11. After 250 metres enter the wood on the right for about 10 metres to a clear rack. Turn left on this for 600 metres until you reach a double gate. Turn right on to a wide track for 1 km. to reach a road.

2. Turn left and walk to a road junction. The crossing road here is the beautiful Lime Tree Avenue (D).

3. Continue straight ahead for a further 800 metres, passing a cricket ground on the left, to reach another junction.

4. Bear right towards Clumber Car Park (refreshments and toilets), past the remains of Clumber House (E) and the well-preserved Clumber Chapel (F).

REFRESHMENTS

The Stables, Clumber House   Meals and snacks.

INTEREST

A. DUKE'S RIDING SCHOOL   This was the second largest riding school in the world, and for a time was also used to house the large numbers of people attending the Welbeck Tenants' Agricultural Society luncheon.

B. WELBECK ABBEY   See Notes on Section 14. **PRIVATE – NO PUBLIC ACCESS.**

C. WELBECK TUNNEL   The Robin Hood Way follows the line of the 1¼-mile (2 km.) long tunnel from South Lodge to the stables at Welbeck, passing under the Abbey itself. The tunnel was built by the 5th Duke of Portland, who developed an exaggerated shyness in later years. The tunnel still remains, dry and well-ventilated, but closed. It enabled the Duke to travel in his coach from his home almost to the edge of Worksop without being seen. Incidentally, the Duke also built numerous underground rooms at Welbeck Abbey.

D. LIME TREE AVENUE (or Duke's Drive)   This is a beautiful 3-mile long drive lined by double rows of lime trees, the finest in Europe. It led originally to Clumber House.

E. CLUMBER HOUSE   The former seat of the Dukes of Newcastle (under-Lyme, not on-Tyne), this immense house was built in 1770 and was one of the most magnificent houses in Europe. It was finally demolished in 1938 and only the stables remain.

F. CLUMBER CHAPEL The private chapel of the family of the Dukes of Newcastle, built in 1884, fortunately still remains intact. It has some lovely wood carvings and rich fittings, and is nearly perfect in proportion.

G. CLUMBER PARK, through which our route passes, is the 3700-acre estate of the Dukes of Newcastle, now owned by the National Trust, and is one of the finest parklands in the County. There are innumerable paths and rides through the woods, as well as walks around the beautiful Lake, which is spanned by a fine classical bridge, from which there is an unforgettable view of the Chapel. Among the facilities are an information centre and shop, restaurant, cafeteria and toilets, as well as cycle hire in summer. The north-east entrance, at Apleyhead Lodge, has a grand classical screen and gateway leading to Lime Tree Avenue. The Park is open at all times and there is an admission and parking charge for cars.

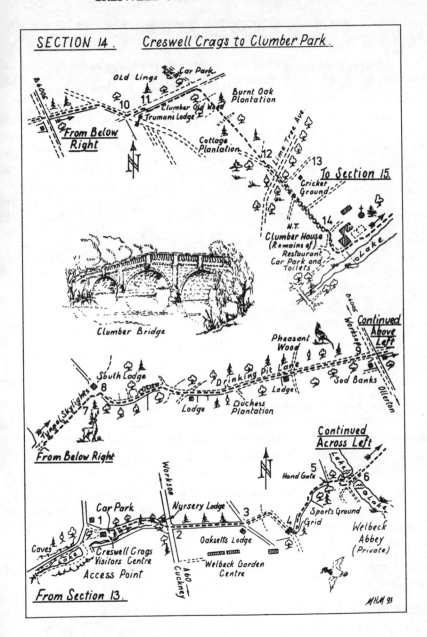

15. CLUMBER PARK TO HAUGHTON

Distance: 10 km. (6.25 miles.)

Maps: Landranger Sheet 120.   1:25,000 Series Sheet SK.67.

Start: Main Car Park in Clumber Park.

How to get there: By road – Follow A.614 northwards to the Apley Head Lodge Gate, signposted entrance, and drive for approx. 3 km. along Lime Tree Avenue then turn left down the road leading to the main Car Park adjacent to the site of the former house of Clumber.

By public transport – for local bus services, enquire from the 'Bus Hotline' Tel. Nottm. 240000.

THE ROUTE

1. From the main car park walk down to the lakeside and turn left along a well-maintained path. Follow Lincoln Terrace along the lakeside for 1 km. and at the end bear left, then right on a clear path through the trees to a handgate under a small stone arch. Go through the arch and cross the next field to another handgate, and go through it.

2. Now turn right and follow a clear bridleway winding through trees, with a fence on the right, eventually coming back to the lakeside some 400 metres on. Continue along the lakeside and through trees to a T-junction, with a footbridge to the right.

3. Turn right over the bridge, pass the head of the lake and reach another junction.

4. Turn right on a clear wide track, still along the edge of the lake.

Some farm buildings now appear on your left. Turn left just past these buildings and go along a short stretch of path between hedges to a small car park t Hardwick Grange (A).

Public toilets are available here.

From the car park bear right towards a signpost for 'Village Hall and Lake', ;noring a road to the left, then bear right again along a metalled road to a ford.

Cross the ford by the footbridge, pausing to look right at the attractive weir nd the fine trees, with waterfowl on the river. A little way along the road after he ford take a bridleway going diagonally left across a field to emerge through a ate on to a minor road.

Turn left and go to the Normanton Gate entrance to Clumber Park, leading •n to the A.614 opposite the Clumber Park Hotel.

0. Through the gate turn immediately right on a path running parallel to the oad, to come out in front of more gates, Drayton Gates.

1. Turn left and cross the busy road to the bridleway opposite, passing the emains of a gate, on to a well-defined track, West Drayton Avenue (B).

2. Go ahead along this green avenue, ignoring side turns. After 450 metres the ane is grit-surfaced and reaches a clearing with a wire fence on the left-hand orner and then an open field.

3. After emerging from the trees head for the distant power cables, then where a track comes in from the right, turn LEFT at a footpath sign and cross a field, following the power cables, aiming for a gap in the woods ahead.

14. Enter the wood and continue following the power cables along a grassy track, to the far side of the wood.

15. At the far side, bear slightly right for a few metres, then go left along a wider track, across a clearing, to a ford in the River Poulter. This is Crook Ford (C).

16. Cross the ford by the footbridge on the left and continue along the track for about 150 metres to a metalled road on the right.

17. Turn right up this, going up a small hill.

18. Where this road turns right into a farm, turn left by pylons, with hedge on the left, for about 180 metres to a junction with a concrete road.

19. Continue ahead along the concrete road, following pylons, and go to the to of the hill by a housing estate, turning right into Brough Lane and headir straight towards the buildings of Bevercotes Colliery (D) which are now visible.

20. Beyond the houses, where the road starts to turn left, take a footpath to th right, with a fence on the left, dropping downhill to the River Poulter.

21. Cross the river by the footbridge and continue ahead to a clearing, then for left into a short stretch of heathland.

22. At a T-junction turn left into another plantation, to another T-junction..

23. Turn right at this junction, along an obvious grassy track curving slightly le to leave the plantation by a red brick house 'Beggar's Rest'. Continue along th track up a small hill and under power lines.

24. At the top of the hill this track meets a wide tarmac track, which is We: Drayton Avenue again. Cross the Avenue and pass through a gate, then con tinue along the track curving right, around farm buildings.

25. At the front of the farm buildings turn left along a gravelled track. (If yo keep straight ahead at this point, a track leads into the red-brick village o Bothamsall). The gravelled track goes between wire fences to a road, B.6387, at gateway.

26. Cross the road, go through another gateway and continue along anothe wide track, passing a wood on the left, crossing the River Meden and goinç under a railway bridge. Then continue ahead to pass a farm (E) on your righ and then cross the River Maun.

27. On the far side of the River Maun, the main track bears left. From this poin the Robin Hood Way turns left (Section 17).

To reach the Access Point for Section 17 at Haughton, turn right at the Rivei Maun and go to the far side of the field, step left for a couple of metres, then resume your original direction to head for a railway bridge. Pass under the bridge to the car parking area on the Walesby to Gamston road B.6387, on the south side of the bridge over the River Maun, 2 km. north of Walesby.

REFRESHMENTS

The Robin Hood Inn, Elkesley   Bar Meals.

Clumber Park Hotel, on A614 opposite the Normanton Gate   Restaurant. Bar meals.

INTEREST

A. HARDWICK GRANGE   This is a purpose-built settlement for Clumber estate workers, built about the same time as Clumber House.

B. WEST DRAYTON AVENUE   This old road, constructed to connect Clumber House with West Drayton, is a public right-of-way in parts, but private in other parts.

C. CROOK FORD   An attractive but deep ford on the River Poulter. Vehicular access from either Bothamsall (Redhill Lane) or Elkesley (Coalpit Lane).

D. BEVERCOTES COLLIERY   This colliery commenced production in 1967. It was the world's first push-button pit and at the time the most modern. Its future, however, became very uncertain during the 1992 recession and at the time of writing this Guide has still not been decided.

E.   The farm stands on the site of HAUGHTON HALL, which was the imposing family seat of the Holles family, the Earls of Clare, who eventually became the Dukes of Newcastle. The Second Duke of Newcastle, nephew of the first Duke, abandoned Haughton in 1770 and it fell into ruins. Nothing now remains except for a few stones incorporated in the farmhouse.

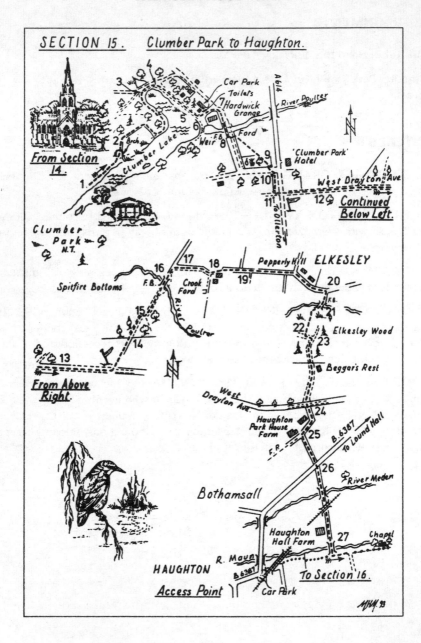

SECTION 15. Clumber Park to Haughton.

16. HAUGHTON TO WHITEWATER BRIDGE

Distance: 5 km. (3.5 miles.)

Maps: Landranger Sheet 120.   1:25,000 Series Sheet SK.67.

Start: North side of River Maun near Haughton Hall Farm. The Access Point for drivers is the parking area on B.6387, Walesby to Gamston road at Haughton, on south side of the bridge over the River Maun, about 2 km. north of Walesby village. M.R. 680728.

How to get there: By road – From A.1 turn on to B.6387 about 1 km. south-east of Elkesley and proceed along B.6387 to parking area. From A.614 take minor road to Walesby about 2 km. north of Ollerton roundabout, then turn left at junction with B.6387 at the Carpenters Arms and proceed to parking area.

By public transport: For local bus services, enquire from the 'Bus Hotline', Tel. Nottm. 240000.

THE ROUTE

The parking area is just off the route of the Robin Hood Way. To reach the Way, take the clear track from the parking area, going under a railway bridge and following the south bank of the River Maun. At the far side of the first field after the railway bridge, step to right for a couple of metres, then resume your original direction, crossing the next field to reach another clear track coming in from the left. This track from the left is the route of the Robin Hood Way.

1. On the direct route from Section 16, bear left on the track for a short distance.

(If coming from Haughton Access Point, keep straight on for a short distance.) There is now a track going to the right, which should be taken. (An interesting detour at this point is to keep going straight on for about 400 metres to the ruins of St. John's Chapel (A), then return.) The track now goes slightly downhill towards a wood. Continue beyond the wood to the bottom of the hill, where the track turns left.

2. Turn left with the track and walk for about 30 metres to a stile in the hedge on the right. Cross this stile, go through the hedge and enter a field. Follow the headland of this field with a stream on your left, as far as the remains of a crossing hedge.

3. Turn right, still following the headland, now with a hedge on the left. Where this hedge turns left, go diagonally left across the field, heading for where a power line crosses a junction of tracks. (Note, in the not-too-distant future there may be a diversion at this point, along two grassy tracks, but this will be waymarked.)

4. Having crossed the field you will meet a grassy track. Turn left along this track until you reach the overhead power lines.

5. The grassy track, which now goes ahead, goes into Walesby village, where refreshments may be obtained. However, our route turns right to follow a headland path with a hedge on left, which goes under two power lines and heads towards a line of houses.

6. On reaching a hedge bordering a road, just before the houses, turn right inside the hedge and go for 100 metres, passing a gap in the hedge, and come to a bridleway sign.
N.B. The route thus described is now the official right-of-way, the route shown on some O.S. Maps having been officially diverted.

7. Turn left at the sign and cross the road, then enter a well-marked narrow lane at another bridleway sign (to Conjure Alders), with barbed wire on the left and a hedge on the right, for about 800 metres, to reach a broader track.

8. Turn right and cross a mineral railway line by a bridge, then continue on a farm track with field boundaries on the right, under 3 sets of power lines.

9. Two fields beyond the last power line, turn right along a lane coming from Walesby (Forest Lane), go through gate posts and then turn immediate left on a well-marked path.

10. At a T-junction with another path coming in from the left, the Robin Hood Way turns right – see Section 17.

To reach the Access Point for Section 17 at Whitewater Bridge, turn left at point 10 above and go due south, at first along the edge of a plantation on the right, then along a field edge, soon to find the River Maun coming close on the right. Here in a low cliff bordering the river is Robin Hood's Cave (B). Several paths now continue southwards, all reaching a plantation on the left, then continuing to another plantation and an exit by a gate leading on to the minor road from the A.614 to Walesby, 2.5 km. from Ollerton crossroads.

REFRESHMENTS

Carpenters Arm, Walesby (on B.6387)   Bar meals, snacks.

INTEREST

A. ST JOHN'S CHAPEL   The tiny, overgrown ruins of the former chapel of Haughton Hall, close to the footpath, are the sad remains of a delightful Norman building, now in a serious state of decay and further threatened by mining operations.

B. ROBIN HOOD'S CAVE   This name is given to a small cave in the outcrop of Bunter Sandstone near Walesby International Scout Camp. The rock forms a low cliff on the bank of the River Maun. It is, to be honest, difficult to conceive of the cave sheltering Robin Hood, or indeed anyone, unless it has suffered from erosion by flooding over the centuries.

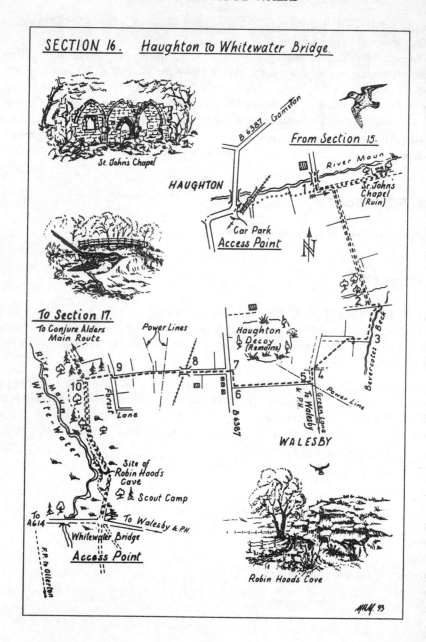

SECTION 16. Haughton to Whitewater Bridge.

17. WHITEWATER BRIDGE TO HAZEL GAP

Distance: 9.5 km. (5.9 miles.)

Maps: Landranger Sheet 120.   1:25,000 Series Sheet SK.67 and SK.57.

Start: On bridleway between Whitewater Bridge and Conjure Alders. The Access Point for Section 18 for those not coming along the Robin Hood Way is the car parking area on the side of the minor road from the A.614 to Walesby, near Whitewater Bridge. The minor road turns off the A.614 about 2.5 km. north of Ollerton crossroads.

How to get there: By road, turn off A.614 about 2.5 km. north of Ollerton crossroads, on the minor road signposted Walesby. The parking area is on the side of this road, at a bend about 1 km. east of the A.614.

By public transport: For local bus services, enquire from the 'Bus Hotline', Tel. Nottm. 240000.

THE ROUTE

Whitewater Bridge is not on the direct route of the Way. To reach the route from the car parking area, take a bridleway signposted Bothamsall & Thoresby. The path goes north with a plantation on the right, slightly uphill at first. Shortly there are several paths all going in the same direction, any of which may be used. Then the River Maun, on the left, approaches the path. The outcrop of Bunter Sandstone forming a low cliff on the river bank contains Robin Hood's Cave (A). Continue in the northerly direction to the edge of a wood to your right. At this point a bridleway comes in from the right. This is the route of the

Robin Hood Way. Continue from point 1 below.

1. If coming along the Robin Hood Way, turn right at the T-junction (i.e. keep straight on if coming from the car park), and follow the path into the woods. The path is well-defined.

2. Shortly after passing a field clearing on the right, bear slightly left at a junction of paths, with a ditch on the left. The copse on the right is part of Conjure Alders (B).

2. When the path reaches the bank of a river (actually the confluence of the Rivers Maun and Meden), bear round to the right along the bank for a few metres to a footbridge. (There is another footbridge further ahead, from which a track leads to Bothamsall village.)

4. Turn left over the first footbridge and follow the clear track over a second bridge and out of the trees into a field. Continue along the waymarked bridleway around the edge of the field, with the hedge always on the left. This bridleway has several turns and is always close to the hedge.

5. Where the bridleway goes through a gap in a crossing hedge to a minor road, go across this road and continue in the same direction through a gate and along another field edge, hedge on left.

6. On reaching the corner of a plantation, DO NOT be tempted to walk just inside the trees, though this appears to be a clearer track, but keep outside the plantation along the field edge.

7. Where the plantation juts out, go right with it for a few metres, then left, to resume the previous direction.

8. Towards the far side of the third field from the minor road in point 5, the trees then out and the main road A.614 appears on the left.

9. A little further on, look for a wide gap in the scrub to the left, by a gatepost. Turn left here, then turn right just before reaching the road and follow the grass verge northwards, this verge usually being kept clear by the County Council.

10. After following this verge for about 900 metres, on the other side of the road, and straight opposite the minor road to Bothamsall, you will see a large green metal gate. Cross the main road here carefully, but DO NOT go through the green gate. Instead take the signposted bridleway starting from the lay-by just to the right of the gate, and join a wide clear track through the woods on the edge of Clumber Park. (DO NOT take the narrow metalled road running parallel on your left. This is private.)

11. Follow this clear track (Freeboard Lane) in a south-westerly direction for about 2.5 km., following its curves but ignoring all side turns, to reach a Lodge (South Lodge) with fine metal gates.

12. Cross the wide track going to the right into Clumber Park at the Lodge and keep to the left of the fence bordering the Lodge garden. Continue in this direction for about 650 metres until a clearing appears on the left, with other tracks going away to the left (most of them telling you that you are entering private property, which, of course, you will not do.) Keep straight ahead still, ignoring these side turns, and shortly the track joins wide green 'ride' through the trees.

13. Continue along this 'ride' for 2 km. to a small area used as a car park, at the side of a road (B.6005). Cross the road. DO NOT go through the gate opposite, at the side of another Lodge (Duncanwood Lodge), but go to its left on to a fenced-off path along the side of a field, still keeping roughly in the same direction as before.

14. Continue ahead along the narrow path for 300 metres, where it bears right to join the main track from Duncanwood Lodge. Go to the left along the track for 1 km. to reach the junction of tracks at Hazel Gap.

REFRESHMENTS

Clumber Park Hotel, on A.614 opposite Normanton Gate   Restaurant, Bar meals.

INTEREST

A. ROBIN HOOD'S CAVE   This name is given to a small cave in the outcrop of Bunter Sandstone near Walesby International Scout Camp. The rock forms a low cliff on the bank of the River Maun. It is, to be honest, difficult to conceive of the cave sheltering Robin Hood, or indeed anyone, unless of course, it has suffered serious erosion form flooding over the centuries.

B. CONJURE ALDERS The bridge on our route, across the Rivers Maun and Meden, crosses at a point which was once 'Coningswath' – of Scandinavian origin and meaning 'King's Ford'. This was on the old 'King's Road' between Blyth and Wellow, and used to mark the eastern boundary of the hunting forest. The name Conjure is a combination of Coningswath with 'Alder' after the alder trees which grow in the copse to the right. The alder flourishes in wet conditions and has been much used for wooden poles and posts, chair legs, clogs, and broom heads, also in gunpowder making and for medicinal purposes.

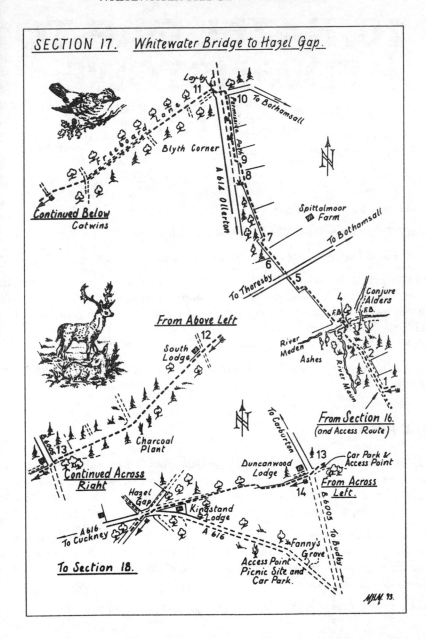

SECTION 17.   Whitewater Bridge to Hazel Gap.

Lay-by
11
10 To Bothamsall
Freeboard Lane
Blyth Corner
Perimeter Park
9
8
Continued Below
Catwins
A 614 Ollerton
Spittalmoor Farm
To Bothamsall
7
6
To Thoresby
5
4
Conjure Alders
F.B.
F.B.
From Above Left
12
South Lodge
River Meden
Ashes
River Maun
2
1
From Section 16.
(and Access Route)
Charcoal Plant
To Carburton
13
Car Park & Access Point
Continued Across Right
Duncanwood Lodge
13
From Across Left.
Hazel Gap
14
B 6005 To Budby
Kingstand Lodge
A 616 To Cuckney
A 616
Fanny's Grove
To Section 18.
Access Point Picnic Site and Car Park.
MHM. 93.

18. HAZEL GAP TO EDWINSTOWE CHURCH

Distance: 7.5 km. (4.7 miles.)

Maps: Landranger Sheet 120.   1:25,000 Series Sheet SK.57.

Start: Hazel Gap, on A.616 about 4 km. east of Cuckney village.

How to get there: Take A616 (Ollerton to Sheffield road) and park at the Forestry Commission Car Park and Picnic Site at Fanny's Grove, about 400 metres N.W. of the triangular junction between A.616 to Hazel Gap (there is at present no footpath link between Fanny's Grove and Hazel Gap). There is also limited parking on a small cleared area on the north side of A.616 at Hazel Gap.

By public transport: For local bus services, enquire from the 'Bus Hotline', Tel. Nottm. 240000.

THE ROUTE

1. On reaching the road (A.616) at Hazel Gap, cross to the south side of the road and take the track opposite, through a gateway and along a clear track with a plantation on the right, in a south-westerly direction. (This is the reverse direction to that described from point 11 in Section 12 to the end of that Section.)

2. After about 550 metres there is also a plantation on the left. Just before reaching the far side of this plantation, turn left on a path through the trees, curving slightly left, then right, to reach a road at a double white gate by a house (Gleadthorpe Lodge).

3. Go through the handgate, cross the road, and take the track on the far side,

hich is metalled.

150 metres after crossing a bridge, do not take the green 'ride' through the ees just to your right, but follow the metalled track for 500 metres to meet a avel track.

Turn left along this track, climbing at first through the forest, to where the ees on the left stop and there is a junction of paths.

Turn right and go across Budby South Forest, ignoring any side turns, for out 2 km., to a junction of wide paths. On the far side of the path which goes ft to right, and slightly to your left, is a large tree. This is Centre Tree (A).

. Turn left, pass double gates and continue down a stony track, again ignoring de turns. Eventually another track comes in from the left and joins our route at red waymark post. Continue ahead, following the red waymarks. At the next nction of paths, ignore all other waymarked tracks and continue ahead, to each the fenced-off Major Oak (B).

. Turn right at Major Oak and follow blue waymarks to Sherwood Forest isitor Centre (C). Then follow signs to the Car park and continue straight cross the centre of the Car Park to a path which heads towards a church spire ow visible through the trees. This is Edwinstowe Church, Continue along this ath, passing a cricket ground on your right, to reach another car park, then eep in the same direction along the pavement to the entrance to Edwinstowe hurch (D).

At this appropriate point our route ends. We hope you have enjoyed your walk.

REFRESHMENTS

Robin Hood's Larder', Sherwood Forest Visitor Centre   Snacks, light meals and refreshments.

Maid Marian Restaurant, Edwinstowe   Meals, snacks.

INTEREST

A. MAJOR (or QUEEN) OAK   The largest oak tree in England, perhaps in the world, this famous tree has withstood lightning, the drying-out of its roots, and even a recent fire. The hollow trunk has a circumference of 32 feet and the spread of its branches makes a ring 260 feet round. The cavity in the trunk is feet in diameter and it is said that Robin Hood (and some of his men) used to hide here. The tree has had to be fenced off to preserve it – the combined weight of the many thousands of visitors was compacting the soil around it, so that water could not penetrate to the roots.

C. SHERWOOD FOREST AND VISITOR CENTRE   Much has been written about this most famous woodland, so we will content ourselves with a very few notes. In the Middle Ages, 'Forests' included woodland, agricultural lands, villages and even whole towns. Sherwood extended from Conjure Alders to Wellow, south to the Dover Beck, then to the Trent at Nottingham, north via Wilford and Annesley to Mansfield, then via Warsop to 'Coningswath'; – about 100,000 acres. What is now known as Sherwood Forest is a 450-acre woodland mostly oak, to the north and west of Edwinstowe. After the Forest ceased to be a royal hunting forest in mid-17th century, large areas were cleared. Many older trees are now hollow and others have a bare appearance at their tops due to rotting, giving them the name of 'stag-headed oaks'. There are other species of trees and bushes in the present forest, as well as an abundance of animal, bird and insect life. For further reading, consult the bookshop at the Visitor Centre which was established by Notts. County Council, and also has a restaurant and exhibition about the Forest and Robin Hood. In the summer, film and slide shows and talks are held at weekends, details of which can be obtained from the Centre, along with numerous leaflets and other sources of information. The Forest Rangers are based here.

D. EDWINSTOWE CHURCH   The church of St. Mary was mentioned in Domesday Book. The present church was begun about 1175 and has a fine 'broach' spire. Inside the church is the 'Sherwood Forest Measure', the 'foot' measure used for measuring forest lands – it is 1½ feet long! According to legend Robin Hood married Maid Marian in the church. Edwinstowe or Edenstou, is a very ancient royal village, named after Edwin, King of Northumbria in the 7th century. A local Guide is published and the village has refreshment and accommodation facilities.

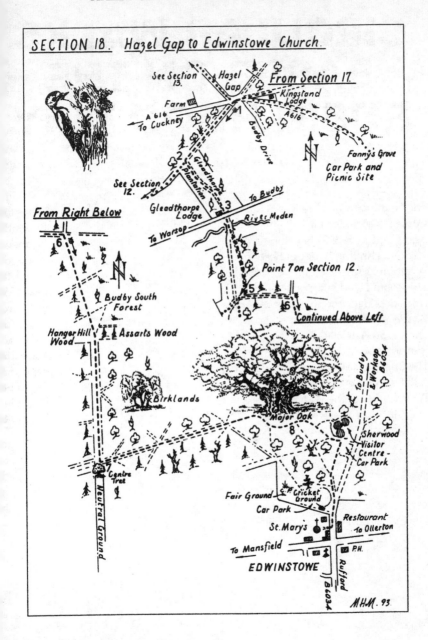

SECTION 18. Hazel Gap to Edwinstowe Church.

See Section 13.

Hazel Gap

From Section 17.

Farm

Kingstand Lodge

A 616 To Cuckney

A616

Budby Drive

Fanny's Grove Car Park and Picnic Site

See Section 12.

Gleadthorpe Plantation

Gleadthorpe Lodge

To Warsop

To Budby

River Meden

From Right Below

Point 7 on Section 12.

Budby South Forest

Continued Above Left

Hanger Hill Wood

Assarts Wood

To Budby & Worksop

B6034

Birklands

Major Oak

Sherwood Visitor Centre - Car Park

Centre Tree

Neutral Ground

Fair Ground Car Park

Cricket Ground

St. Mary's

Restaurant To Ollerton

To Mansfield

P.H.

EDWINSTOWE

Rufford

B6034

M.H.M. 93.

CIRCULAR WALKS BASED ON THE ROBIN HOOD WAY

THE HEMLOCK STONE WALK

. varied walk taking in the intriguing Hemlock Stone, Stapleford Hill, giving
iews of three counties, the Nottingham and Erewash Canals and the Bramcote
{ills.

)ISTANCE   Short Route: 3 miles (5 km)
                                  Long Route: 6.25 miles (10 km)

)URATION   Short Route: 2 hours
                                  Long Route: 3 hours

;TART   Bramcote Hills Car Park, Corner of Coventry Lane (A6002)
                                  and Ilkeston Road (A6007). Grid Ref. SK 501386.

/IAPS REQUIRED   Landranger 129
                                  Pathfinder SK43/53 SK44/54

{OW TO GET THERE BY CAR   A52 Nottingham-Derby road. At the Sherwin
\rms Public House take A6007 signposted Ilkeston.

{EFRESHMENTS   Jaguar Public House, Hickings Lane, Stapleford
                            Trowell Garden Centre
                            Festival Inn, Trowell
                            Bramcote Manor Public House

{. From the car park, pass through the small opening into Coventry Lane. Cross
:he road and walk up the Lane to the entrance way onto the open space of the
{emlock Stone/Stapleford Hill.

?. Take the path climbing up hill to the Hemlock Stone.

{. At the Stone you have a choice, either to walk up to the 'long point' of
;tapleford Hill, or to take the path around the hill. To walk to Stapleford Hill
;ummit follow the path to the rear of the Hemlock Stone, that climbs uphill
through a wooded area. Retrace your steps back to the Stone, and then take the

signposted path on your right (approx 120° turn) leading around the edge of the hill.

4. Continue through the wood bearing left at each junction until you reach the meadow area. Continue through to the field where you turn right into a second field.

5. Turn left and follow field edge path towards the railway line to reach a stile.

6. Over the stile, turn left on the wide path at the foot of an embankment going through a copse.

7. At a fork, bear right, climb uphill then follow the path turning right then left towards houses, car park and fence. **Do not** go through the gate but turn right following the fence at first, then into a narrow twitchell. **Unprotected railway line not far ahead, so keep children and dogs close to you.**

8. Cross railway line with **great care**, then over the stile bear left across the field to another stile and junction of paths.

If you are taking the short route, turn right and follow instructions from Section 26. If following the long route, turn left returning to this point later in the walk.

9. Follow perimeter fence of Trowell Garden Centre (refreshments available in the cafe).

10. Passing the entrance to the Garden Centre, cross the road and follow the marked path to Swansea Bridge.

11. You leave the Robin Hood Way at Swansea Bridge by dropping down to the towpath on the near side of the canal and then turning left towards Trowell.

12. At the end of the towpath go down some steps, under the M1 bridge, then climb up steps back onto the canal.

13. Continue along the towpath going under a roadbridge (Nottingham Road Trowell) and continue along a canal now filled in and landscaped as a Linear Park. Continue for 800 metres to reach the footpath on the left.

14. Leave the canal path, descend steps and continue along track to reach Stoney Lane.

15. Turn left along Stoney Lane and continue to reach Ilkeston Road near railway bridge.

16. Turn right, walk over the railway bridge, cross the road with **great care** and ke the footpath up the lane (The Forge).

7. Walk to the end of The Forge to reach a stile and field gate, then cross 2 further tiles.

8. Enter a grass meadow then aim for the large factory with a tall chimney seen head. After walking so far across the meadow, a green bridge comes into view. Aim for this.

9. Cross the bridge and walk along the track to the Erewash Canal.

0. Turn left along the towpath for 500 metres to reach the Lock.

1. Turn left and leave the canal, going over a railway bridge, then through a gateway continuing along a marked path to a bridge. Then forward under the railway to reach Ilkeston Road, Trowell.

2. Turn right over a pelican crossing. Drinks and food are available at the Festival Inn. Visit St. Helen's Church.

3. Walk up Nottingham Road to rejoin the Canal.

4. Return along the footpath, going under the M1 then up to Swansea Bridge.

5. Leave the canal, return to Trowell Garden Centre and take the path around the Garden Centre to rejoin the short route. Continue along the towpath for .6km to reach Coventry Lane.

6. Cross the road, take the path opposite going under the railway bridge and continue until you reach Moor Lane. Turn right along Moor Lane and leave the wood to follow a well-marked track with playing field to the right. On reaching the T Junction, rejoin the Robin Hood Way.

7. Continue straight on for 50 metres, turn right and take the footpath.

8. Follow the footpath towards the first stile (you can leave the path here to visit Bramcote Manor for food and refreshments). Over the stile, then immediately over a second stile on the left, still following the boundary of the sports field.

9. Climb up the hill to enter a wood. You are now on the Bramcote Hills. Take a diagonal path to the right, still climbing, to reach a path junction after 70 metres.

0. Bear right, and follow the boundary fence to a quarry on the right. Keep parallel to the fence and take a left turn signposted Bramcote Park Car Park and drop downhill to reach the end of the walk.

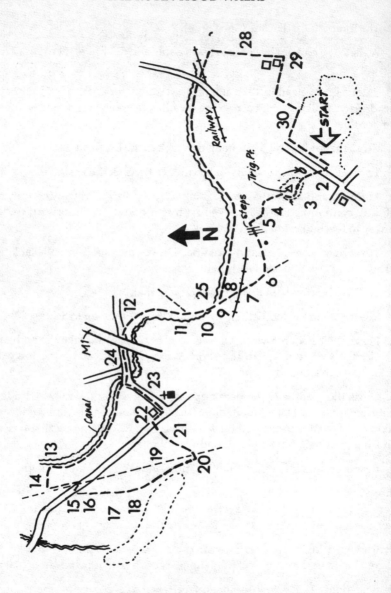

THE HEMLOCK STONE WALK

COSSALL,
A SECLUDED OASIS

A peaceful stroll to an undiscovered area starting at the beautiful village of Strelley, and visiting Catstone Hill with distant views of Wollaton Hall, Cossall and Babbington.

DISTANCE	5.75 miles (9 km)
DURATION	3 hours
START	Strelley Village, park on grass verge just past Church. Grid ref. SK 505421.
MAPS REQUIRED	Landranger 129 Pathfinder SK44/54

HOW TO GET THERE BY CAR From M1 Junction 26 to Nuthall Island, then outer loop road (B6004) to traffic lights. Turn right into Strelley Village.

REFRESHMENTS Broad Oak, Strelley
Gardeners Inn, Awsworth

1. Return up Main Street past the village church, which is well worth a visit. This church was endowed in 1356 by Sir Sampson de Strelley, who lies buried with his wife in an alabaster tomb-chest in the centre of the chancel. Parts of the church date from the 13th Century. Other family tombs are to be found in the church.

Strelley Hall is situated next to the church. Some of the buttressed medieval walls of the old hall have been incorporated into the roadside wing of the 18th Century brick stables of the new hall.

Continue along the road to a sharp bend. Note the stone setts which marked the former Monks' Way and the Cedars of Lebanon trees nearby.

2. Follow the bridleway (Strelley Lane) and continue along the track until you

103

reach a second bridleway on the right.

3. Walk through a box gate and follow the bridleway with excellent views of the rolling countryside and Wollaton Hall. Go through 2 bridlegates to reach a path junction.

4. Then turn right along another bridleway with a hedge on the right. Forward under the M1 motorway, turn left and in 150 metres turn right.

5. Follow the bridleway through 2 further fieldgates. Follow the well-marked track to Cossall Road.

6. Cross the road and take the path opposite going over the stile and continuing until you reach a bridge over the disused Nottingham Canal. Turn right and walk along the towpath for 200 metres to the next bridge.

7. Turn right over the bridge and walk across a field to a stile (Mill Lane).

8. Over the stile and take the path opposite, across a paddock, to another stile in the far end of the field near houses.

9. Turn right on Church Lane, Cossall and walk up to the village church.

10. Retrace your steps for 30 metres to take a track downhill at the side of Church Cottage (the home of Louie Burrows: D. H. Lawrence's fiancee). Continue to a stile in the hedge on the left. Go over this, turn right going downhill over 2 stiles to reach a footbridge. Follow the path uphill through a gateway to reach a path junction with a four-way signpost.

11. Over the stile, turn left and follow the field edge path to the far corner stile. Over this, then along a bridleway for 100 metres to reach the road. (At this point by continuing straight on to the end of the road you arrive at the Gardener's Inn, Awsworth. Retrace your steps to this point).

12. Turn right and walk up Westby Lane (a former railway line) towards Babbington Village. Just before the road forks we reach a path junction. Turn right on path signposted to Strelley. Go across the field to reach the hedge on the left. Follow this until you reach a stile and wood.

13. Over the stile, turn left and follow the field edge path towards Strelley Park Farm. Take the stile shortly before the Farm.

14. Over the stile, turn right and cross 2 meadows to reach a farm track.

15. Cross the track and over a stile. Keep the fence on your right. Almost at the field corner bear left and climb over a stile in the hedge. Head straight across the next field to a stile set about halfway along the boundary of the wood with this field.

16. Follow a well-defined path through Spring Wood. On reaching the far side of the wood, go over an earth footbridge and climb a high stile going across a field to the left of Turkey Fields Farm.

17. Head diagonally left to the far left field corner and over another stile on the right of a field gate. Keep to the right hand fence, following a narrow belt of trees on your right, climbing over 2 stiles close together to reach a bridleway.

18. Turn left, go over the M1 bridge and continue along the track to reach the Main Street, Strelley.

19. Turn right to end the walk. Take the opportunity of looking around Strelley village and take a well-deserved rest at the Broad Oak Inn at the far end of the village.

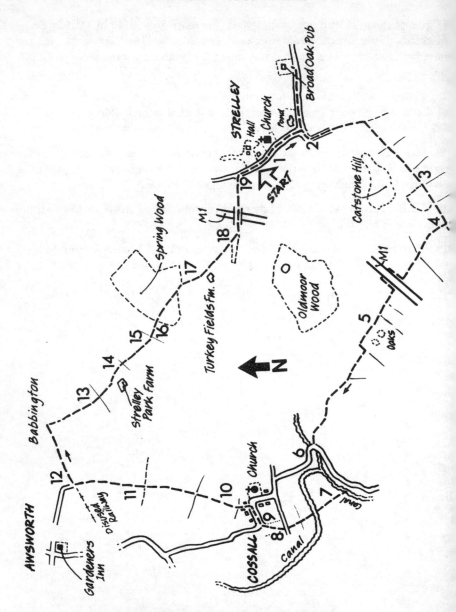

COSSALL, A SECLUDED OASIS

BEAUVALE PRIORY AND ROBIN HOOD'S WELL

surprisingly rural ramble from Greasley Church through beautiful woodlands
nd experiencing one of the best ridgeway paths in the county.

ISTANCE   5 miles

URATION   2½ hours

TART   Park in layby on B600 outside Greasley Church SK490472.

MAPS REQUIRED   Landranger 129, 120
                      Pathfinder SK44/54 and SK45/55

HOW TO GET THERE BY CAR   From Nottingham A610 at Nuthall Island take
B600 to Greasley Church. Exit 26 M1 to Nuthall Island A610, take B600 to
Greasley Church.

REFRESHMENTS   Horse and Groom public house, Moorgreen

. From the car park walk along the roadside towards Nottingham as far as
Greasley Castle Farm. Cross the road at its entrance and go over stile opposite.

. Follow the field edge path and climb up the hill, over a second stile and up to
he top corner (signpost). Excellent views from this point.

. Turn right and walk along a field edge path, going into another field as it
ends left, then walk to the corner of this field, turn right again and walk down
o a further signpost.

. Turn left and through the gap in the hedge, keep a straight line beside the
hedge until reaching a stile and small bridge.

5. Cross over stile and walk towards the right hand corner of the field ahe where there is a bridge crossing the Giltbrook.

6. Cross the bridge, turn left and follow edge of field to reach a stile in part the fence ahead. This is the source of the Giltbrook by the stone wall. Ke straight on through the gap in the hedge, then turn sharp right and walk to t corner of the field.

7. Over the stile, turn left onto New Road and continue along the road to rea the edge of a wood with a finger post directing you to Hucknall, Annesley a Underwood.

Before doing this, however, take the opportunity of looking at the site Beauvale Priory. Walk a further 120 metres to the bend in the road seen ahea Look over the hedge to see the remains of Beauvale Priory with a farmhouse ar buildings. The remains are on private land.

Beauvale Priory was one of only 9 Carthusian monasteries in England, and is th second best preserved, having been dissolved in 1539 after Robert Lawrence, th Prior, was imprisoned for refusing to acknowledge Henry VIII as Head of th Church of England. He and the ex-prior became the **Beauvale Martyrs** whe they were executed as traitors in 1535. They are commemorated in an annu service held on the site of the monastic church. Note the large wall and traces a fine church window. The remains are on private land. Return to the footpa sign.

8. Climb over the stile and follow a wide track at the side of a plantatio Continue beyond the wood to a field hedge at the side of the M1 motorway. the 3-way wooden finger post, turn left and follow the track to enter the woo Follow the woodland path seen ahead until it reaches a stone surface path.

9. Turn right at this point and follow the track, which soon turns left, continu to climb uphill to a junction where 5 paths meet.

10. Walk straight on, following a narrow forest track to reach the wood edg where you will meet a further stile. The view from this point is sensationa Savour it for a few minutes.

11. Turn left, following a wide track beside Morning Springs Wood. After abou 800 metres, where the track turns right across the field, our path continues alon the edge of the wood as far as a row of oak trees. Follow the path on the right the oaks and cross the grass to a stile.

2. Follow the well-surfaced bridleway by turning left and go into High Park Wood. Continue along this for nearly 1.5km, where it joins a metalled road. Continue along this to reach the B600 at Beauvale Lodge. (To view the reservoir, turn right for 50 metres.)

3. Pass through the gateway and turn left along the main road. Follow this through the outskirts of Moorgreen to reach the Horse and Groom public house.

4. Cross the road (signposted to Eastwood) and follow this until you reach a finger post on the left hand side in 200 metres.

5. Follow the footpath to Greasley Church through a farm, cross two fields to enter the graveyard of Greasley Church.

6. Walk to the Church, visit the grave of Benjamin Driwater (Captain Cook's surgeon) and look over the wall to observe the remains of Creasley Castle.

Greasley Castle Farm was originally the site of a fortified manor house belonging to the Cantilupe family. They commenced building their first house on the site in around 1341. Some of the moat and stone walling survive, and a ruined wall and reconstructed pointed arch were incorporated in the existing farm building, which dates from around the 18th Century.

Return to car park at the church gate entrance.

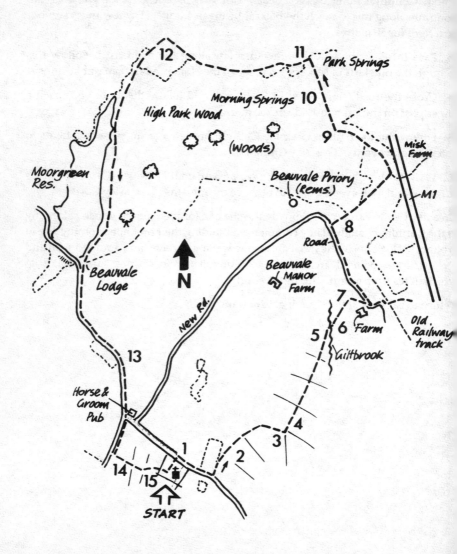

BEAUVALE PRIORY & ROBIN HOOD'S WELL

THE OLD HUNTING LODGE OF BESTWOOD

A chance to walk through the Bestwood Country Park on recently reclaimed paths close to the centre of Nottingham.

DISTANCE   5 miles (9 km)

DURATION   2½ hours

START   Winding House Car Park, Park Road, Bestwood Village Grid ref. SK537476.

MAPS REQUIRED   Landranger 129
Pathfinder SK44/54

HOW TO GET THERE BY CAR   From Nottingham, A611 to Bulwell Forest then B683 to Bestwood Village, then right turn onto Park Road, Bestwood.

REFRESHMENTS   Bestwood Hotel
Bestwood Lodge Hotel

1. From Car Park retrace your steps down Park Road passing the Bestwood Hotel and walk to a crossroads.

2. Turn left, cross Moor Road and walk 300 metres, passing houses, to reach a low wall on the far side of a railway embankment. Step over the wall on your right, ascend steps up the embankment, then bear right to enter Bestwood Country Park (Bestwood Lakes Site) at a footbridge over the River Leen.

3. There is now a choice of routes across the Park:

3a. One is to cross and follow the path leading up a low hill, then going right along a clear track along the ridge with a plantation to the left. Later this track

111

bears right again and drops to a stile leading to a narrow road where you turn right. This is the **Recommended Route** as it gives better views of the Lake.

3b. The other route is to turn right just before the footbridge and follow a clear winding track beside the Lake. This eventually leads to a house and a metal gate and stile, leading to the narrow tarmac road reached in 3a.

From both routes, follow the narrow road to its junction with B683 opposite a telephone kiosk.

4. Turn left along B683, crossing the road, then almost immediately turn right along a street called The Spinney. Follow this street round until you see the end of the cul de sac.

5. Just before the end of the street turn left onto a signposted path between houses. This path then climbs uphill with a hedge on the left and eventually a new housing estate on the right. Continue along the path to reach a stile. Over the stile, cross 2 fields to reach Park Road. Your car is parked to the right if a short walk is required.

6. Continue ahead along the road bearing right to enter Bestwood Park and eventually reach Alexandra Lodge.

7. Take the path to the left of Alexandra Lodge and climb up a sandy path for 30 metres. Turn right downhill to take the left turn up Main Drive. Continue along Main Drive ignoring all turn offs to reach a farm gate and box stile.

8. Walk straight ahead, passing the first locked entrance to reach a second entrance, right, to enter Big Wood. (If you would like refreshments, do not enter the wood, but continue ahead for 400 metres to reach Bestwood Lodge Hotel. Afterwards retrace your steps to the entrance of Big Wood.)

9. Take the track through Big Wood and continue until reaching a left hand junction. Note 2 large houses through the trees on the boundary of the Park.

10. Turn left and take the path that continues along the boundary of the Park. Ignore the first right turn but some 50 metres after this turn right out of the Wood onto an open grass area. Turn left and follow the path parallel to the previous path.

11. Follow this as it contours around the former colliery spoil heap. From here excellent views are obtained of the City of Nottingham, Hucknall and afar. The path brings you back to the Winding House Car Park.

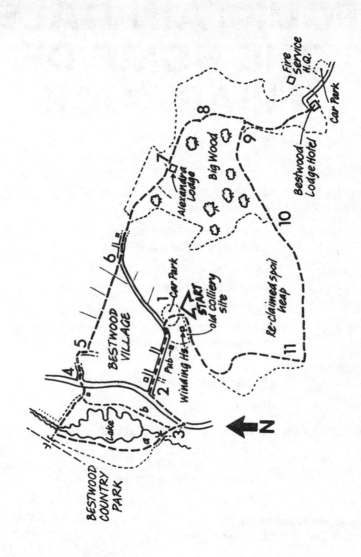

THE OLD HUNTING LODGE OF BESTWOOD

FOUNTAIN DALE, THE HOME OF FRIAR TUCK

A stunning woodland walk in the heart of outlaw country, passing the site where Robin Hood met Friar Tuck in Fountain Dale.

DISTANCE   Short Route: 2.5 miles (4.5 km)
Long Route: 6.5 miles (10.4 km)

DURATION   Short Route: 1.5 hours
Long Route: 3.5 hours

START   The Greenwood Craft and Garden Centre, Portland College for the Disabled. Grid Reference SK550567. (A60 Mansfield–Nottingham Road)

MAPS REQUIRED   Landranger 120
Pathfinder SK45/55

HOW TO GET THERE BY CAR   From Mansfield and Nottingham A60.

REFRESHMENTS   Greenwood Craft and Garden Centre
Black Bull, Blidworth
Bird in Hand, Blidworth
Little John Inn, Ravenshead

1. Leave the Craft Centre Car Park, cross the access road and take the track opposite past buildings to come to marker posts with white tops. These mark the route to follow on the Friar Tuck Trail.

2. Continue along the track parallel to the A60 trunk road seen through the plantation on the right. On reaching the bend in the track our route joins the Robin Hood Way coming in from the right.

3. We turn left and follow a marked path across partly wooded heathland for 1km until you reach a crossroads with telegraph wire above.

4. Continue straight on to the first of the Fountain Dale Lakes. This is also the location of Friar Tuck's Shelter. Continue for 200 metres to meet a path coming in from the left.

We have now joined Blackscotch Lane (should you wish to continue on Friar Tuck's Trail follow the description from paragraph 18 – this is the **shorter route**.)

5. The longer route passes just to your right between 2 wooden posts, then you turn left again to resume in the same direction for 400 metres, winding among trees.

At the end of the Lake, the path splits into two. Take the left fork, drop down and cross a small ditch with the outflow of the Lake on the right, then continue ahead across a large open field, keeping the stream to the right.

6. After 500 metres, turn right at a crossing of bridleways, go through trees and over the stream into a field, then up a rise to Providence Farm.

7. Walk straight on, keeping the Farm and then the hedge to your left.

8. Go through a gate at the end of the hedge and turn right along the farm drive to its junction with a road.

9. Turn left along the road, and follow the road for 400 metres to where it bears left.

10. Take an unmetalled lane straight ahead at the bend (New Road) for about 1.3km to reach the junction just before Norwood Hill Farm. We now leave the Robin Hood Way route.

11. Turn right and walk down another track to a junction of paths, turning left past a children's play area to reach houses. Turn right and walk up to the main road. Turn right again and walk up the street passing several public houses to St. Mary's Church.

12. After visiting the Church, take the road opposite (Rickett Lane) and walk 80 metres to a foot path left at the side of Woodstock Cottage.

13. Over the stile and walk through the garden then go over a further stile into a hedged track. Follow this to another stile. You now enter a field, walk straight onto another stile.

14. Cross the field aiming for the hedge opposite. Cross the stile, turn left and walk to the corner of the field. Over this stile, walk out of the overhanging hedge, turn right and walk down the hill to the stile in the right hand corner of the field.

15. Over this stile and walk across 2 more fields. Note the Druid Stone.

16. Walk uphill straight across the next field to a further stile seen at the top of the rise. Over this stile, drop downhill in a straight line, then climb up the bank and cross 5 fields following a similar course. When reaching a large open field turn right to follow a headland path and aim for the plantation seen ahead and the corner of the field and a further stile.

17. If refreshments are required, drop down the hill to the Little John Public House at Fishpool (Ravenshead). Our route, however, continues right uphill to reach a road.

18. Cross the road and take the bridleway opposite, drop down hill going into a wood to reach a junction as stated in paragraph 4. Turn right and walk to next junction to Blackscotch Lane.

19. Turn left along Blackscotch Lane and walk up to the next junction (follow marker posts with white tops on Friar Tuck's Trail).

20. Rejoin the shorter route and turn left along zig-zag path to enter the outbuildings of the Portland Training College. Walk straight on down the driveway, past buildings to arrive at the start of the walk.

FOUNTAIN DALE, THE HOME OF FRIAR TUCK

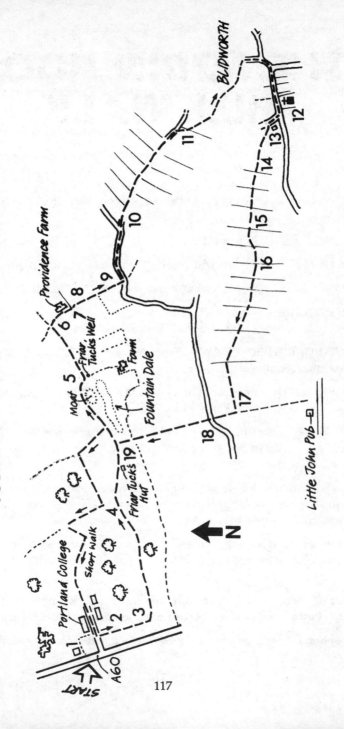

THE ROBIN HOOD HILL WALK

Retrace Robin's footsteps to enjoy the magnificent view from this well-known viewpoint.

DISTANCE   7 miles (11 km)

DURATION   3 hours with option: 2½ hours without option

START   St. Michael's Church, Farnsfield. Grid Ref SK645565

MAPS REQUIRED   Landranger 120
                      Pathfinder SK65/75 (Newark West)

HOW TO GET THERE BY CAR   From Nottingham A614 to White Post Inn, then Mansfield/Southwell Road.

REFRESHMENTS   Red Lion, The Plough and The Wheatsheaf Public Houses, all at Farnsfield

1. From St. Michael's Church, walk towards crossroad opposite Red Lion Public House. Turn left down Blidworth Road and take footpath at the side of the wall to The Hall and new properties.

2. Forward through double gates to cross 2 fields, half left to enter a hedged track. In 200 metres veer right at a T junction and after just over 1 km turn half left across an arable field to enter Coombs Wood, seen ahead.

3. Just inside the Wood follow the path to the right, then as you leave the trees walk up the hill to the right of the Wood to join a hedged cart track (Rob Lane). Turn left.

4. After 200 metres, at a footpath sign, the walker has the option to make a short detour to Robin Hood Hill, one of the finest viewpoints in Nottinghamshire.

If the **option** is taken, turn right, follow the hedge line for 300 metres, bear left and at the gap in the hedge go right for 150 metres to footpath sign, where you turn left to meet a minor road. Cross to the gate opposite, following the track until it bears left, then half right to the foot of a copse. Follow the headland path, keeping the trees on your left, to reach a stile. Over this, ascend half left to the summit to enjoy the view.

To return to the main route, just retrace your steps to the footpath sign on Rob Lane (point 4).

5. If coming from Robin Hood Hill turn right, or if this option is not taken, keep straight along Rob Lane to arrive at a track coming in from the left. Ignore this, turn right and go into a sunken path to reach the road opposite Wood Farm.

6. Turn left along Greaves Lane and in 400 metres turn left again opposite Meadow Farm. We now leave the Robin Hood Way on a footpath, pass through a gate and forward for 100 metres, then turn right in the next field to the corner where you turn left keeping the hedge on your right. After 50 metres go through a gap in the hedge, turn left and ascend the hill now with the hedge on your left. At the top of the field follow the hedge to the right and in 200 metres turn left, as waymarked, through another opening.

7. Walk downhill, with Farnsfield in the distance, continuing straight ahead to climb slightly to a stile. Continue in the same direction across another field to a stile which gives access to a newly set plantation. Take the clear path between the trees forking right to enter Farnsfield Football Club ground via a gate.

8. Walk down the left hand side of the pitch, passing the changing rooms, to join a track. Where this turns left, take the stile on the right and continue with the hedge on the right to the end of the meadow. Turn right over a stile to enter a hedged ginnel which leads onto the main road opposite the Plough Public House in Farnsfield.

9. Turn left along Main Street to return to St. Michael's Church and the end of the walk.

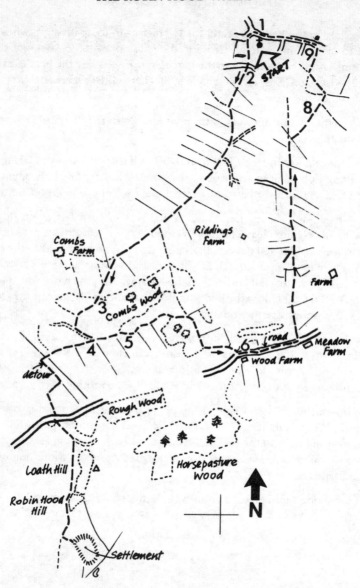

THE ROBIN HOOD HILL WALK

NORWOOD HALL: AND THE BRAMLEY APPLE

A recommended walk through Norwood Park, with its stately home and extensive orchards and some quiet and attractive villages.

DISTANCE   7.25 miles (11.5 km)

DURATION   3.5 hours

START   Kirklington Station, Southwell Trail   Grid Ref. SK 675665

MAPS REQUIRED   Landranger 120 (Mansfield & The Dukeries)
                    Pathfinder SK65/75 (Newark West)

HOW TO GET THERE BY CAR   Take the minor road for 1 mile SW of Kirklington. Kirlington is situated on the A617, 10 miles NW of Newark.

REFRESHMENTS   Admiral Nelson Westhorpe, public houses in Southwell, Old Reindeer Public House Edingley.

1. From the car park, follow the Trail past the former Statin House and continue towards Southwell. After about 2km you reach a road crossing the track. This leads to Maythorne.

2. Our route turns right along a minor road to reach a main road. Turn right for 100 metres, then turn left to enter the grounds of Norwood Park.

3. Follow the track into the Park to arrive at a crossroad junction. Go over the stile to follow a wide grass track. You have a beautiful view of Norwood House, home of Sir John and Lady Victoria Starkey.

4. On reaching the Halam Road cross it to enter a field opposite. Head across the field aiming just to the right of a brick house seen ahead.

5. On reaching the B6386, if you need refreshments turn left and walk to the Admiral Nelson seen just down the road. Our route continues across the road to enter a twitchell which leads to Westhorpe.

6. Cross the road half right to go up a second twitchell which leads to a small paddock. Cross the bridge and go right to a kissing gate. Pass through a group of attractive houses to a road, turning right and going round the corner to cross the field to the left.

7. Turn right to rejoin the road going uphill to reach the B6386. Follow the road opposite (Saversick Lane) past some ancient willows. You are now joining the Robin Hood Way. Turn left into the drive of the first house reached called 'Halam Gate'. Follow the fence on the left through the garden, over a stile into an orchard. Walk straight across the field to reach another stile.

8. Cross the stile, turn right and drop down into Halam to visit the Church and have refreshments.

9. Walk back up the lane (Radley Road) past the Church and walk up to a path just short of the left hand bend in the road and Manor Farm.

10. Take the path on the right which goes behind Manor Farm and past the tennis courts to a footbridge. Cross 2 stiles then turn right uphill past Machin's Farm. Continue straight ahead along the edge of fields to reach a lane.

11. Cross Newhall Lane and continue ahead up Turncroft Lane. After 200 metres take a path on the right and follow the edge of 2 fields passing New Hall Farm. This is the highest part of the walk with excellent views. Continue downhill through the remains of an orchard to reach Greaves Lane.

12. Turn right along Greaves Lane for 1 km to reach a field gate on the left just after the road junction on the right. Cross 2 fields, then go through a cottage garden to reach Edingley Main Street.

13. Turn left past a road junction to reach a footpath on the right just before the village Church and the Old Reindeer Public House (some 100 metres away).

14. The path follows the Edingley Beck over several fields to reach the Southwell Trail. Turn right on the track to reach the car park.

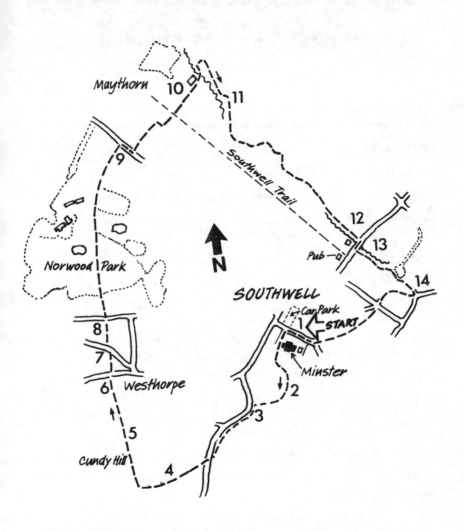

NORWOOD HALL, AND THE BRAMLEY APPLE

WATERMILLS AND ORCHARDS

An easy ramble around Southwell in the shadow of the historic Minster.

DISTANCE   4.75 miles (7.5 km)

DURATION   2.5 hours

START   Church Street car park, Southwell   Grid Ref. SK 602539

MAPS REQUIRED   Landranger 120 (Mansfield & The Dukeries)
Pathfinder SK65/75 (Newark West)

HOW TO GET THERE BY CAR   A617 and A612 from Newark. B6386 from
Nottingham and Mansfield.

REFRESHMENTS   Admiral Nelson, Newcastle Arms and many others in
Southwell.

1. From Car Park cross the road and walk up to the Minster, passing the West
Front. Continue straight on passing the Bishop's Manor and along a lane to the
War Memorial and the archway to the Park.

2. Pass through this and follow the avenue of lime trees beside the sports field,
then left down to the Potwell Dyke and a path swinging right to reach Nottingham Road.

3. Turn left and walk 300 metres to cross the road and take the bridleway.

4. This begins as an overgrown lane then goes along the edge of 2 fields. In the
second field, go right through a gateway (Curdy Hill).

5. This path follows a hedge and then descends an open field with a fine view of
a tree-lined 'Dumble' and beyond it Westhorpe. Descend to a bridge over the
Dumble, then cross a small grass field to another footbridge. Walk up a hedged
twitchell to the main street.

6. Cross half right to another twitchell which takes you to Oxton Road (the Admiral Nelson is to the right if refreshments are required).

7. Cross the road and go straight across an arable field to a stile and Halam Road.

8. Cross this road and take the path opposite into the orchards and grounds of Norwood Park, owned by Sir John Starkey. Our path continues in a northward direction passing between fruit trees and arable land, with a fine view of Norwood Hall on the left. After the orchards carry straight on the estate road to reach Kirklington Road.

9. Turn right, then left after 100 metres (road signed to Maythorne). Follow this road to reach the Southwell Trail. An option is available from this point to turn right along the Trail.

10. Our route continues into Maythorne, going past the Mill and former mill cottages to take a path over a bridge at the rear of the Mill. Turn right following a stream to a further stile.

11. You now follow the River Greet into Southwell along the winding course of the river going across several fields and stiles.

12. On reaching the road at Cauldwell's Mill, now converted to flats, turn right to reach the Newcastle Arms where we join the end of the Southwell Trail (shorter option).

13. Cross the road to enter Riverside and go down steps to rejoin the River Greet path. Follow this pleasantly landscaped path to the Newark Road.

14. Turn right in front of a former railway cottage and take the path on the right. Follow this path with the Potwell Dyke on your left and enter a cul-de-sac of a new housing development. Turn left and go ahead when the road swings away. Cross Kirklington Road to the footpath beside the dyke, forward with a conifer hedge on your right, then bear half right to a fence on your left, which you follow for 150 metres to a stile to emerge onto Shady Lane.

15. After crossing this, the Minster comes once again in sight in all its glory. You have only to cross one meadow to Church Street, and right to return to the car park.

Be sure to take time to visit the medieval Minster and its exceptional Chapter House.

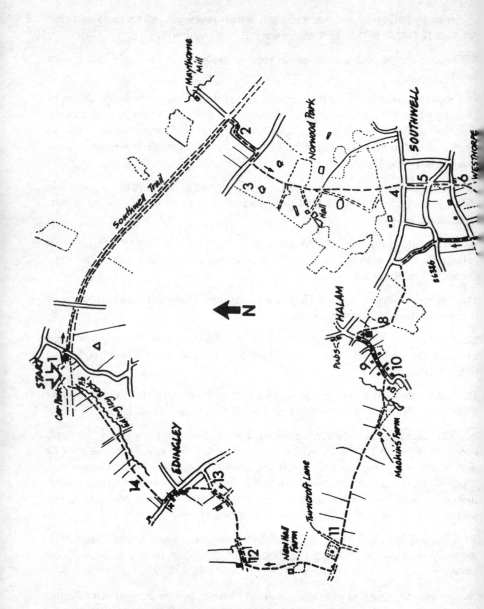

WATERMILLS & ORCHARDS

THE PULPIT ASH WALK

Discover the historic site where William Mompesson, plague Rector of Eyam, held his services in Eakring. Also visit Mansey Common.

DISTANCE   6.25 miles (10 km)

DURATION   3 hours

START   Savile Arms, Eakring (please park at the top of the car park) Grid Ref. SK 672623

MAPS REQUIRED   Landranger 120 (Mansfield & The Dukeries)
Pathfinder SK66/76 (Ollerton) & SK65/75 (Newark West)

HOW TO GET THERE BY CAR   Turn east off the A614 4 miles south of Ollerton roundabout to Eakring village.

REFRESHMENTS   Savile Arms, Eakring

1. Our route follows the Robin Hood Way by turning right from the car park then left and right into Church Street. Go straight ahead at the next bend to follow a wide track around a double bend to reach the site of the Pulpit Ash on the right, over a plank bridge.

2. After visiting Pulpit Ash (Mompesson Cross) take the stile opposite and cross the field with a hedge on the left to reach a further path. Turn right and follow the track to reach another stile, then a narrow path between hedges to come onto Side Lane. Walk straight ahead to the road junction.

3. Turn right, walk up the road for 350 metres, ignoring the Robin Hood Way path, to go past a farm to the next corner in the road. Take this road straight ahead (Brail Lane) walking past a cottage to reach a bridleway sign on the left.

4. Continue uphill on the bridleway to reach a further track (on a clear day it is possible to see Lincoln Cathedral from this point). Turn left to reach a road.

5. Turn right along this road for 400 metres past Coultas Farm to reach a path on the left and entrance to Dukes Wood.

6. Follow a well-defined track through attractive woodland ignoring the track on the left to Dukes Wood Nature Trail. Keep straight along the track passing the occasional 'nodding donkey' until you reach Whitestub Lane.

7. Enter the wood on the right and follow a narrow path through trees to soon rejoin the route of the Robin Hood Way on the right coming from Kirklington. Ignore this, but continue straight on through the trees to reach a plank bridge at the end of the path.

8. Cross the plank bridge on your left and keep to the right hand edge of field along the outer edge of Roe Wood.

9. Near the end of this wood go over a small dyke with waymarks, turn right, still along the outside of the wood.

10. Where the wood goes sharp right turn left across a large field, over a bridge and head across a further field to reach the boundary fence of Holywell Farm.

11. Over the stile turn left and head over a second stile, then across 3 fields to reach Orchard Wood Farm. Pass between the left hand side of the farm and barns, go ahead to the next field.

12. Follow its edge by turning right, descending to a footbridge then across 2 large fields to reach Dilliner Wood.

13. Straight ahead through the trees to reach Mansey Common.

14. The way now is not very clear, but in fact bears left (NNW direction) for about 450 metres to a footpath sign.

16. Turn right at this sign, and follow a clearer path, winding through scrub and waymarked at intervals until you reach a footbridge.

17. Cross the footbridge and climb the bank on the far side. At the top of the bank go left for a few metres with the hedge on the left, then strike to the right, across the field keeping parallel to power lines about 45 metres to your left and descend to a crossing farm track.

18. At the farm track go left for a few metres, then right, over a plank bridge, then slightly left towards a gap in the far hedge.

19. At this gap cross a cart bridge and continue ahead up a rise to the corner of a hedge.

20. Keep ahead with the hedge on the right, descending to reach a grassy track. You leave the Robin Hood Way at this point by turning right and crossing 2 fields with the path then edging down into woodland along the bank of a stream. Join the road at the bottom of Church Hill, and continue ahead past 3 large beech trees to the next corner.

21. Turn left along Sandy Lane (a hedged green lane). At a fork turn right and continue until you reach a point where there are stiles on both sides of the lane.

22. Take the left hand stile, veer right across the field to a further stile and cross this stile. Turn left and follow the road to return to the Savile Arms Public House.

THE PULPIT ASH WALK

RUFFORD ABBEY AND LAKE

A former Cistercian Abbey of Rufford with its beautiful lake and grounds, former King's hunting ground at Pittance Park, a gentle walk along the River Maun and a visit to the capital of Sherwood Forest at Edwinstowe.

DISTANCE	5.5 miles (9 km)
DURATION	2.5 hours
START	Rufford Country Park, Main Car Park
	Grid Ref. SK 644647
MAPS REQUIRED	Landranger 120 (Mansfield & The Dukeries)
	Pathfinder SK66/76 (Ollerton)

HOW TO GET THERE BY CAR   A614 from Nottingham

REFRESHMENTS   Robin Hood Inn
Dukeries Hotel
Rufford Abbey

Start the walk from the car park and walk towards the Abbey Buildings.

1. Turn left past the Abbey walking along a tree-lined 'L' shaped walk. At the end turn left past the lake.

2. Cross the bridge on the right and follow the path round the lake. (A detour is possible by crossing the bridge on the left to the Mill just before reaching the road in Rufford where the tourist information and exhibitions are held.)

3. The walk continues across the road, with the mill cottages to the right and the ford across the road to the left. Forward along a headland path for 1.25 km to reach the main A614 road.

4. Cross the road carefully to a stile which leads to a path alongside the railway.

Cross the footbridge, then cross a stile to the left and turn right to follow the edge of several fields going into a track into Edwinstowe.

5. At the road turn right going under a railway bridge, then pass the Dukeries Hotel. In 100 metres turn left into Mill Lane (signed Clipstone).

6. Then 50 metres before a second railway bridge turn right along a path to follow the River Maun.

7. Where the river starts to swing right, we join the Robin Hood Way and take the path to the left and continue to the railway line. Cross the railway line and continue to a road.

8. Cross this road and go straight on following a hedge to reach Holly Farm. Continue down the farm drive to a road B6030.

9. Turn left on the main road and continue for 300 metres towards the traffic lights and a bridleway sign on the right. (The Robin Hood Public House is available for refreshments.) Follow the track across the fields to reach woodland.

10. Pass through the woodland and turn left along the edge, then right down the field edge to a track. Turn left to reach the entrance drive to 'Centre Parcs'. Walk straight ahead for 500 metres ignoring side turns to reach the A614.

11. Cross this road with **extreme care** to turn left on the pavement to reach the entrance to Rufford Abbey. To avoid cars, take a path left beside the bus turning circle, as this brings you onto the main driveway leading up to the Abbey and to the end of our walk.

12. Refreshments, shops, crafts and a pleasant enclosed garden await you in or behind the stable block.

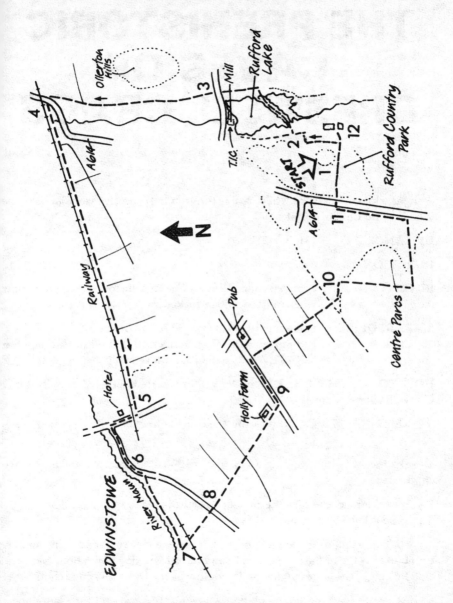

RUFFORD ABBEY & LAKE

THE PREHISTORIC CAVES OF CRESWELL CRAGS

A slightly longer but worthwhile ramble through the extensive woodlands of the Welbeck and Clumber Estates.

DISTANCE   13 miles (21 km)

DURATION   6 hours

START   Creswell Crags Visitors Car Park (before leaving note time when car park will be locked)

MAPS REQUIRED   Landranger 120 (Mansfield & The Dukeries)
Pathfinder SK67/77 (Clumber Park & East Markham) &
SK47/57 (Worksop South & Staveley)

HOW TO GET THERE BY CAR   The Visitor Centre is situated ¾ mile east of Creswell village on the B6042.

REFRESHMENTS   Carburton Cafe (detour to Greendale Oak Public House, Cuckney)

1. Take the wide track leading away from the Visitors Centre to meet the A60 trunk road.

2. Cross the road and take the metalled road opposite, with a bridleway sign. This road is lined with conifers.

3. At a Y-junction near a lodge, go half left along a concrete road going slightly uphill. At the top of the rise bear right and head towards a plantation, taking no side turnings. The large building to the right was the Duke's Riding School.

4. Just before reaching the plantation, cross a cattle grid and turn left along a farm track with a fence on the right. Go through a gate and continue around the outside of the plantation, then descend to a handgate in the corner of the field. The roofs now visible to the right are those of Welbeck Abbey.

5. Go through the gate, bear right for 250 metres, then take the track left, over the end of the Great Lake of Welbeck.

6. Across the next large field is a line of rough land. This marks the line of the Welbeck Tunnel.

This tunnel was built by the 5th Duke of Portland, who was reputed to be disfigured, perhaps by a skin complaint, and never allowed anyone to see him. He built the tunnels, large enough to take his coach and horses, so he could travel about the estate unseen. Entire suites of rooms were constructed under the Abbey, including a huge ballroom.

Follow this across the field, taking care of the circular depressions in the ground. These are skylights and ventilate the tunnel. Most of them are capped with concrete but some are not, so they are best avoided. Having followed this line right across the field, you come into sight of a castellated lodge (South Lodge). Just round the back of this Lodge is the entrance to the tunnel.

7. As you approach the Lodge at the edge of a small plantation on the left is a bridleway sign. Go through a handgate into the plantation, then turn right along the side of a wooden fence to another handgate with a green bridleway sign. On reaching the Lodge turn right onto a sandy track.

8. On the clear track (Drinking Pit Lane) go towards the right keeping the iron fence on your right, through a low sandstone gorge (note the graffiti!) and continue along the track ignoring all side turns, for about 2.5km, passing 2 lodges on the way. The track then meets a road B6005 at Sod Banks.

9. Cross the road, go through a gate and enter another clear track, which shortly meets a tarmac road. Go to the right on this road to an imposing lodge: Truman's Lodge. Note the arched gateway.

10. Our route leaves the Robin Hood Way by going through the archway and walking up towards the pay desk for vehicle entrance into Clumber Park.

11. Opposite this pay desk turn right on a track. We follow this track ignoring all side turns for 2.5km. On reaching a barrier, ignore the left turn but still continue straight on to reach Lime Tree Avenue.

THE ROBIN HOOD WALKS

12. Turn right along this road over Carburton Bridge through Carburton Lodge entrance. Walk up the road to reach the post box.

13. Turn right up a track to Carburton Church and Manor Farm. Turn left opposite the Church and take a footpath at the side of a water course and follow this to reach once again the B6005.

14. Turn left and walk down to a road junction. (A cafe is open in season in the old school premises.) Continue uphill for 500 metres on B6005 using road verge on the right to reach a footpath on the right.

15. Turn right and follow the forest track for just over 1 km ignoring all junctions to reach a gate. Go through this and continue straight ahead to reach a large layby area. This is Hazel Gap.

16. Ignore the path on the left but take the track ahead along an unmaintained country road. Follow it as it curves left through plantations to pass a house, Corunna Lodge, and meet a minor road. This is now Welbeck Park.

17. Turn left along this minor road and pass another lodge – Bentinck Lodge – on your left.

18. Continue along the road to where it bends left at a barrier with a 'strictly private' notice. Bear left with the road and continue into Norton Village, going round a sharp lefthand bend opposite a telephone kiosk.

19. Shortly after the lefthand bend, take the road turning right, signposted Holbeck and Worksop, and continue along it, climbing slightly, to pass the village name-sign.

20. 100 metres after the name-sign go right, over a stile and follow the hedge line to your left across a long, narrow field, to a kissing gate leading onto a road opposite yet another Lodge.

At this point it is possible to make a diversion for refreshments to the Greendale Oak Inn in Cuckney Village by turning left off the road and following a waymarked path. It will then be necessary to return to point 20.

21. Bear left along the road, through a handgate and follow a beautiful tree-lined drive with attractive views, passing Park Lodge on the right after 600 metres and then entering Tile Kiln Wood. Bear right along the main drive, ignoring a minor road from the left.

22. Turn left at the second barrier, along a minor road to the Main Gates Lodge and the A60.

23. Cross the A60 and head towards Holbeck Woodhouse. Ignore the first right turn.

24. Take the second right turn signed 'footpath only' along a lovely avenue of evenly spaced lime trees. This passes St. Winifred's Church on your left, then meets a road in Holbeck village, opposite Hillside Cottage.

25. Turn left, then immediate right on a signposted footpath to Creswell Crags. This runs between hedges to a stile, then with the hedge on the left for 2 fields.

26. At the third field keep ahead between a row of widely-spaced trees on the right and a hedge on the left, to a stile into a fourth field. Cross the fourth field with the hedge on the right and the fifth field similarly.

27. On entering the sixth field continue uphill following a line midway between 2 woods. At the top of the hill aim for a stile at the right hand corner of the field. Cross this stile and continue following a stone wall to the brow of the hill.

28. At the brow of the hill where the wall turns right, go slightly to the left to drop down the slope into the valley of Creswell Crags, crossing a stile at a stone wall and coming to the edge of a stream.

29. On reaching the stream, turn right and continue, keeping the stream to your left, to the far end of a small lake and a 'T' junction.

30. Turn left and proceed to the edge of the road, then turn sharp right and go down a path through a small wood to reach Creswell Crags Visitors Centre and car park.

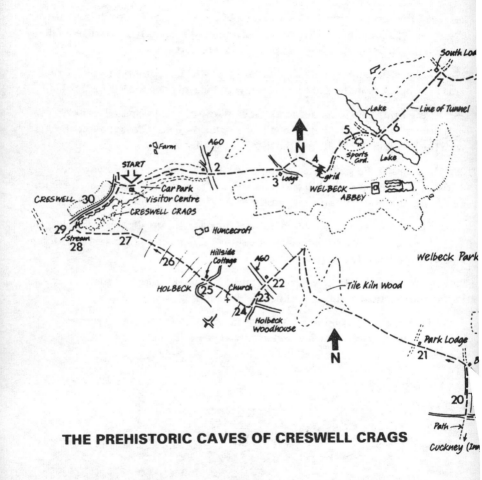

THE PREHISTORIC CAVES OF CRESWELL CRAGS

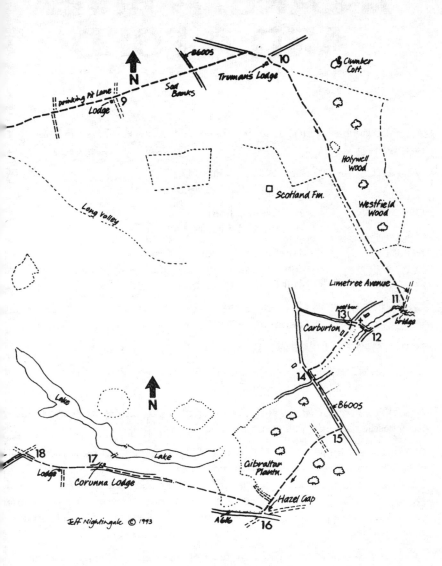

A LAKE, A RIVER
AND A FORD

A gentle ramble around Clumber Lake, alongside the River Poulter to the picturesque Crookford.

DISTANCE   Short Walk: 3.5 miles (5.6 km)
                      Long Walk: 9 miles (14.5 km)

DURATION   Short Walk: 2 hours
                      Long Walk: 4.5 hours

START   Main Car Park, Clumber Park
                      (note: entrance charge to park your car, unless you are
                      National Trust Member)

MAPS REQUIRED   Landranger 120 (Mansfield & The Dukeries)
                      Pathfinder SK67/77 (Clumber Park and East Markham)

HOW TO GET THERE BY CAR   from Nottingham take A614

REFRESHMENTS   Clumber House (National Trust)
                      Clumber Park Hotel

1. Walk down from the car park to Clumber Lake by turning right and following the lakeside path until you reach Clumber Bridge.

2. Walk over Clumber Bridge. If you are following the **short route** turn immediately left and walk along the road at first to reach the car park, then go through bar gate and continue along a clear path at the side of the lake until you reach woods, then the weir, over which you cross a bridge to reach Hardwick village (the short route joins the long route at this point, follow description from here at paragraph 16.)

2a. If you are following the **long route** cross over Clumber Bridge, cross the road and take the road signposted to South Lodge.

. Continue along this road for 1.2 km to reach South Lodge.

. Go through the fine metal gates of South Lodge to join the route of the Robin Hood Way. Turn left along Freeboard Lane. Continue along this path for 2.4 km o reach the A614.

. Just before the main road, in front of a crossing ditch follow a track left hrough the woods to come out at Drayton Gates (entrance to Clumber Park).

. Turn right and **carefully** cross the A614 main road. Go through a clearing, ast the remains of a white gate, onto a well-defined track called West Drayton Avenue.

. Go ahead along the green avenue, ignoring side turns. After 450 metres the ane is grit surfaced and reaches a clearing with a wire fence on the left hand orner and an open field.

. A track eventually comes in from the right. Turn left here at a footpath sign and cross a field, following power cables, aiming for a gap in the woods ahead.

. At the far side, bear slightly right for a few metres, then go left along a wider rack, across a clearing, to a ford in the River Poulter. This is Crookford (ideal lace for a rest).

10. Carry on uphill on a tarmac road passing a bridleway and Robin Hood Way ign on the right, to reach a further bridleway on the left.

11. Turn down the track passing Crookford Farm and keep on a well-defined rack over open fields (woods on the left are called Spitfire Bottoms). Continue ahead to join with and pass through another conifer plantation still keeping to a well-defined path.

12. We continue along the track to eventually reach the bank of the River Poulter (a delightful spot). The path is now easily followed towards Clumber Park which can be seen ahead.

13. On reaching a bridlegate at the roadside of the A614, cross the road with care to enter a further plantation. Go through a gate and follow a well-defined path through the wood keeping to the edge of the wood. On reaching the far end of the wood, walk straight ahead along the field edge path to reach a gap in the hedge onto a tarmaced road.

14. Keep left to go along the road, through gates into a fruit farm. Continue on a

grass track across the fruit farm to reach a gate into Hardwick Grange (if you have time, have a look around the village).

15. Turn left and walk 50 metres to reach a car park and to join the Robin Hood Way. Turn right at this junction and walk forward to reach Clumber Lake and toilets. You also join the short walk at this point, coming in from the left across the weir.

16. Turn right and follow the path around the lake, returning to Clumber House and Church. (You will be walking the Robin Hood Way in reverse, keep to waymarked route.)

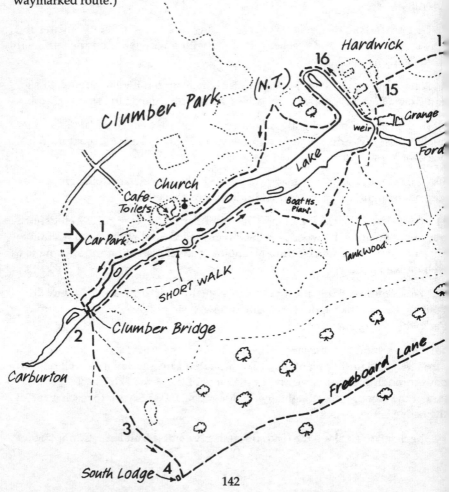

142

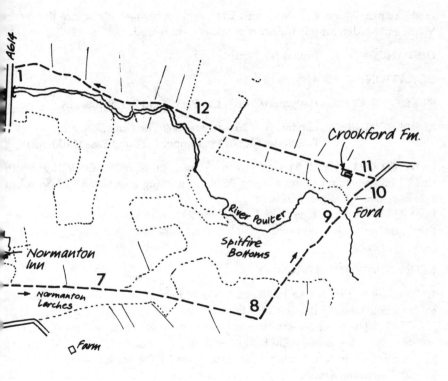

A LAKE, A RIVER & A FORD

THE MEETING OF THE WATERS

Find Conjure Alders and the King's Crossing, an historic site where the rivers Maun and Meden meet in the heart of ancient Sherwood.

DISTANCE	8 miles (12.9 km)
DURATION	4 hours
START	Haughton Corner Car Park. Grid Ref. SK 680728
MAPS REQUIRED	Landranger 120 (Mansfield & The Dukeries)
	Pathfinder SK67/77 (Clumber Park and East Markham)

HOW TO GET THERE BY CAR   from A1 turn on to B6387 about 1 km south east of Elkersley and proceed along B6387 to parking area GR 680728 on south side of bridge over River Maun, or
from A614 take minor road to Walesby about 2 km north of Ollerton roundabout, then turn left at junction with B6387 at the Carpenters Arms and proceed to parking area.

REFRESHMENTS   Walesby village

1. From the car park take the track towards railway going under bridge and across 2 fields following the River Maun to reach a bridleway and join the Robin Hood Way. There is now a track going to the right which should be taken. (An interesting detour at this point is to keep going straight on for about 400 metres to the ruins of St. John's Chapel, then to return.) The track now goes slightly downhill towards a wood. Continue beyond the wood to the bottom of the hill, where the track turns left.

2. Turn left with the track and walk for about 30 metres to a stile in the hedge on the right. Cross this stile, go through the hedge and enter a field. Follow the headland of this field with a stream on your left, as far as the remains of a crossing hedge.

Turn right, still following the headland, now with a hedge on the left. Where is hedge turns left, go diagonally left across the field, heading for where a power e crosses a junction of tracks (Note: in the not too distant future there may be a version at this point along 2 grassy tracks, but this will be waymarked.)

Having crossed the fields you will meet a grassy track. Turn left along this track til you reach the overhead power lines.

The grassy track, which now goes ahead, goes into Walesby Village, where freshments may be obtained. However, our route turns right to follow a adland path with a hedge on the left, which goes under 2 power lines and heads wards a line of houses.

On reaching a hedge bordering a road, just before the houses, turn right inside e hedge and go for 100 metres, passing a gap in the hedge and come to a idleway sign.

.B. The route thus described is now the **official right of way**, the route shown some O.S. maps having been officially diverted.

Turn left at this sign and cross the road, then enter a well-marked narrow lane another bridleway sign (to Conjure Alders) with barbed wire on the left and a edge on the right, for about 800 metres, to reach a broader track.

Turn right and cross a mineral railway line by a bridge, then continue on a farm ack with field boundaries on the right, under 3 sets of power lines.

Two fields beyond the last power line, turn right along a lane coming from alesby (Forest Lane). Go through gate posts and then turn immediate left on a ell-marked path.

. At a T-junction, we turn left towards Whitewater Bridge going due south, at rst along the edge of a plantation on the right, then along a field edge, soon to nd the River Maun coming close on the right. Here in a low cliff bordering the ver is Robin Hood's Cave. Paths continue south to Whitewater Bridge but we turn to junction with bridleway coming in from the right.

. Continue straight on and follow the path into the woods. The path is well efined.

2. Shortly after passing a field clearing on the right, bear slightly left at a junction f paths, with a ditch on the left. The copse on the right is part of Conjure Alders.

13. When the path reaches the banks of the river (actually the confluence of t Rivers Maun and Meden) bear round to the right along the bank to a footbrid; We leave the Robin Hood Way at this point and head for the next bridge se ahead.

14. Over the bridge and follow a clear well-marked track which follows t River Meden on the left and a plantation on the right. Take the path that tur right at the end of the plantation and follow the path into Rothamsall Villa (note Motte seen ahead close to the village).

15. On reaching the main street of Bothamsall, turn right going past the pc office and parish hall to reach the Church of St. Peter and Mary.

16. Take the road to the left of the Church, going past Church Farm, a: continue to eventually go into a green lane. Go through 3 farm gates to rea: Haughton Park House Farm, where you rejoin the Robin Hood Way.

17. Turn right along the Robin Hood Way to follow a farm track to the B6387.

18. Cross the road, go through another gateway opposite and continue alo: another farm track under a railway bridge to pass Haughton Hall Farm the cross the River Maun.

19. Turn right, rejoining the original path taken at the start of the walk, a: follow the River Maun and return across the fields to reach the car park.

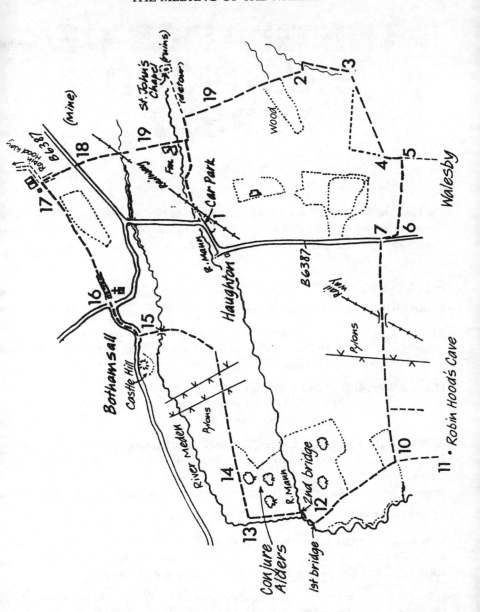

THE MEETING OF THE WATERS

THE GLADES OF SHERWOOD FOREST

The Heart of Robin Hood Countryside, walking in Sherwood Forest, visiting the Sherwood Forest Visitor Centre, Birklands, St. Edwin's Chapel, Archway House, River Maun, Centre Tree and the famous Major Oak. A lot to see and enjoy.

DISTANCE	8½ miles (13.7 km)
DURATION	4 hours
START	Park in one of several car parks at the Sherwood Visitors Centre. In the season there will be a small charge for parking.
MAPS REQUIRED	Landranger 120 (Mansfield & The Dukeries) Pathfinder SK46/56 (Mansfield) and SK67/77 (Clumber Park and East Markham)

HOW TO GET THERE BY CAR Take A614 from Nottingham then B6034 after Rufford Country Park into Edwinstowe. Follow the signs to Sherwood Visitor Centre.
From A1 take A614 to Ollerton Island, then A6075 to Edwinstowe.

REFRESHMENTS Sherwood Visitor Centre

1. From the car park follow the footpath signposted to the Major Oak. Pass the Visitor Centre to its left and continue on the waymarked path. (You may wish to enter the Visitor Centre at this time or later when the walk returns.)

2. Before reaching the Major Oak, a gate appears on the right hand side of the fence you have been following for 500 metres.

3. Turn right and follow the footpath for 800 metres crossing 3 major tracks before reaching the top of a small hill and reaching a fourth track.

4. Go straight on with a plantation on the left to reach a pole gate and the boundary of the Dukeries Training Area.

5. Cross the track ahead then take the footpath towards Budby going diagonally left across heathland following a sandy track for 1km. Keep to this track as this is an army training area, which you have the right to walk through. After 1.2km you will reach a further wide path.

6. Turn left along the path going past Ladysmith Plantation to reach a cross-roads of paths. Carry straight on eventually dropping downhill to rejoin the Robin Hood Way at Hanger Hill junction.

7. Turn left and walk the Robin Hood Way path in reverse following a tarmac drive. After 1.5km you leave this track by going right onto a forest path (refer to section 12, point 6 in main route).

8. Follow this track for 1.3km still on the Robin Hood Way in reverse direction, to arrive at a sharp bend. Our route goes straight on at this point, with the path we have been following going right. You now walk along a green ride to reach a junction at a fire hydrant (yellow) seen on right.

9. Turn left and follow the track crossing a further track and some 150 metres further on step right for about 5 metres to visit the site of St. Edwin's Chapel.

10. Continue along the forestry track with a field boundary seen on the right. This takes you to a main road: A6075.

11. Cross the road and walk down a wide earth track and follow this until you reach the Archway House.

12. Pass Archway House and walk down to the River Maun.

13. Turn left before the bridge, taking a footpath still on the Robin Hood Way in reverse direction. Follow this path along the river bank until you reach a path junction.

14. Go straight on now leaving the Robin Hood Way. Our path goes into a wide track turning left and following on its right the sports field of the Edwinstowe Leisure Centre and a school. Carry on until you once again reach the A6075.

15. Cross the road, turn left going past Villa Real Farm and continue downhill to reach a footpath.

16. Go through a heavy farm gate and continue along the farm track through a further gate into a field and then into a narrow track to reach the forest plantation seen ahead.

17. Walk straight on for 200 metres following yellow waymarks through plantation to reach a further track. Turn right and walk a further 150 metres. Turn left now and walk for 150 metres to reach a wide, stoney track (Centre Tree is 100 metres to the left after going through double gates.) If you visit Centre Tree return to previous junction, and continue straight on ignoring side turns. Eventually another track comes in from the left and joins our route at a red waymark post. Continue ahead, following the red waymarks. At the next junction of paths, ignore all other waymarked tracks and continue ahead to reach the fenced off Major Oak.

18. Turn right and follow blue waymarks to Sherwood Forest Visitor Centre and onto the car park.

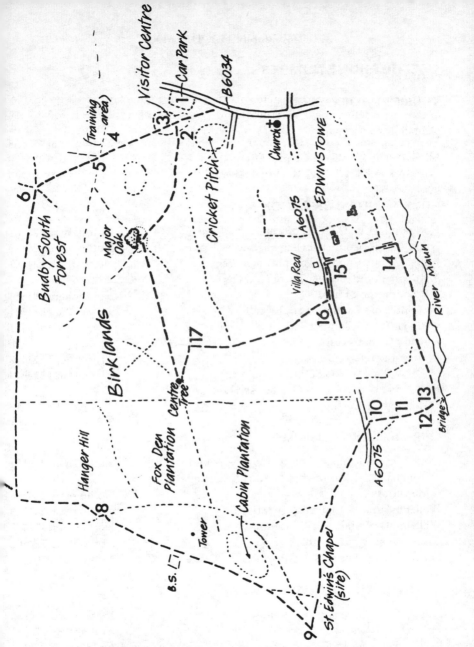

THE GLADES OF SHERWOOD FOREST

USEFUL PHONE NUMBERS

TOURIST INFORMATION

Nottingham, Smithy Row	Nottingham 470661
West Bridgford, County Hall, Loughborough Road	Nottingham 773558
Sherwood Forest Visitor Centre, Edwinstowe	0623 824490
Worksop, Public Library, Memorial Avenue	0909 501148

ADVICE AND INFORMATION

Nottingham City Council Information Office	Nottingham 470661
Notts. County Council, Leisure Services Dept.	Nottingham 823823
Notts. County Council, Footpaths Officer	Nottingham 774483
Nottingham City Council Recreation Dept., Woodthorpe Grange	Nottingham 691666
East Midlands Tourist Board, Lincoln	0522 531521
National Trust, Clumber Park	0909 486411
Forestry Commission –	
Sherwood Office	0623 822447
Thieves Wood Office	0623 822549
Nottingham Civic Society Gatehouse Shop, Nottingham Castle	No Phone No.

LIBRARIES AND MUSEUMS

Notts. County Council, County Library, Nottm.	Nottingham 412121
Nottingham Castle, Brewhouse Yard & Costume Museums	Nottingham 483504
Wollaton Park, Natural History Museum	Nottingham 281333
Wollaton Park, Industrial Museum	Nottingham 284602
Canal Museum, Nottingham	Nottingham 284602
N.C.C. Leisure Services Archivist Record Office	Nottingham 504524

COUNTRY AND OTHER PARKS

Nottingham University Park (Office)	Nottingham 254650
Bulwell Hall Park	Nottingham 278045
Leen Valley Country Park	Nottingham 752661 & 273151
Newstead Abbey (Office)	0623 792822

Rufford Country Park	0623 823148
Clumber Park (National Trust)	0909 486411
Creswell Crags Visitor Centre	0909 720378
Sherwood Forest Visitor Centre	0623 823202
Erewash Valley Area Management	0773 768596
Wollaton Park	Nottingham 282146

TRANSPORT SERVICES

British Rail Passenger Enquiries, Nottingham & Derby	0332 32051
For all Bus Services – The 'Bus Hotline'	Nottingham 240000

MISCELLANEOUS

Papplewick Pumping Station Trust	Nottingham 632938
Lingdale Rural Craft Centre	0623 794858
'Tales of Robin Hood', Maid Marian Way, Nottingham	Nottingham 483284

THE NATIONAL FARMERS' UNION
EAST MIDLANDS REGION
4 St. Mary's Place, Stamford, Lincs., PE9 2DN.

The agricultural pattern in Nottinghamshire can be generally described as being mixed/arable. Many soil types will be found within the county from heavy to light and sandy. Most arable crops can be grown on the soils found in Nottinghamshire, there being extensive acreages of all cereal crops, i.e. wheat, barley and some oats, oilseed rape, sugar beet, potatoes, and some horticultural crops which are found mainly in the south of the county. With the exception of hops and extensive vegetable production, such as cabbages and cauliflowers, most arable crops can be seen in the county. Very few of the county's farms are pure livestock farms, most fall into the category of mixed/arable, with the grassland being leys, i.e. short or medium term grass grown to produce hay and sileage and grazing for dairy beef and sheep animals. While there are a number of dairy and beef herds in the county, by comparison with our neighbours in Derbyshire, the numbers of such enterprises are relatively small. However there are a large number of sheep flocks to be found throughout the county. The farmyards in Nottinghamshire are a true mix of new and old buildings, with many fine examples of traditional farm buildings which have either been adapted to modern agricultural practices or put to some other use.

Putting back Britain's Heart of Oak!

The name of 'Sherwood' is known the world over as the greenwood home of the legendary 'outlaw' Robin Hood. The name conjures up the image of majestic broadleaved forest in the heart of England, with fleeting glimpses of deer in dappled woodland glades.

The reality can be a disappointment to the many thousands of visitors who come to Sherwood each year. Its fame lives on but the forest seems largely to have disappeared. The single stretch of ancient woodland at the Birklands near Edwinstowe, some 500 acres scattered with gnarled and decaying oaks, is often portrayed as all that remains of the wild landscape of the 'Shire wood' which once ran from Nottingham to Worksop, 20 miles long and upto 8 miles wide.

The truth is that Sherwood Forest is still here, but in places its traditional character has been lost or destroyed, leaving many disconnected fragments. Centuries of decline have broken the threads that once bound these surviving pockets of history, culture and ecology into a single cohesive living landscape. The medieval Royal Hunting Forest was a complex blend of woodland, heathland, farmland and settlements, all subject to the special rule of Forest Law - designed to protect the type of countryside which produced good hunting for the King and his favourites.

is not too late to reverse this decline. We can still pick up these reads and start to renew and replace the lost connections in the ndscape. Not to make a fossilised landscape, nor to build a living useum, but to repair the damaged landscape for those who live and ork in it, and for those who come to experience the magic of its story.

o do this the Forestry Commission has launched the Sherwood itiative, an imaginative project to bring Sherwood Forest back from e brink. Working with other key bodies, Sherwood is being looked at n the light of its cultural and ecological history, and in the context of urrent land use questions. By careful adjustment of existing woodland, e addition of carefully planned new tree planting, and the recreation of herwood's traditional heaths, it is possible to redress some of the losses f the centuries and meet the challenges of the changing countryside.

cope will exist for sponsors and supporters of all hapes and sizes to contribute to this process, from ndividuals or local groups to local businesses or najor corporations.

Vant to help?
Vant to know more?
'ontact;

ustin Brady
herwood Initiative
'orestry Commission
'uckney Road
'arburton, Worksop
Jottinghamshire S80 3BP
'el:0909 472965   Fax:0909 482875

Sherwood Forest

(A 'One Minute' History)

Over the last 8 centuries Sherwood Forest has been damaged by constant pressure and subtle changes in land use. The uncleared wilderness of woodland and heathland was declared a Royal Forest in the 12th century, mainly as a hunting reserve for deer and wild boar. At that time the word 'Forest' was a legal designation and the area subject to Forest Law contained areas of heathland, open farmland and some settlements, not just woodland. All deer and other game became the property of the King as did standing timber, and a complex system of fines, taxes and licences grew up to control the use of the forest area.

Over-grazing meant that the area of woodland was gradually reduced and heathland grew in its place, resulting in large open areas of heathland and scrub known as 'forest waste'. This land continued as wilderness, parts of it falling in and out of farming with the changing fortunes of agriculture. The dry sandy Sherwood soil was unsuited to continuous cropping. Gradually, parts of the forest were handed over to the Church and private estates, agricultural techniques improved, and the forest continued to shrink.

Large areas of crown land were subsequently to pass into private hands to form the great estates of the Dukeries. It is on those surviving estates that much of the remains of Sherwood Forest is to be found, although much of this was 'created' during the landscape movements of the 18th and 19th centuries. Other landholdings became more fragmented and the traditional character of the landscape continued to be eroded as agriculture became more intensive, coal mining grew in significance and roads, buildings and development further divided the forest lands.

BUS 'N BOOTS !

take *The Sherwood Forester* →

to the Robin Hood Way

The popular Sherwood Forester network of bus services in Nottinghamshire gives CHEAP and EASY access to the Robin Hood Way at several points on its route, including Burntstump Country Park, Newstead Abbey, Rufford Country Park, Edwinstowe and Sherwood Forest Visitor Centre, Clumber Park and Creswell Crags.

The Sherwood Forester
operates
SUNDAYS and BANK HOLIDAY MONDAYS
LATE MAY - SEPTEMBER and
SUMMER SCHOOL HOLIDAYS

For information on *SHERWOOD FORESTER*
and all other Nottinghamshire Bus Services phone the
Nottinghamshire County Council
Buses *"Hotline"* on Nottingham (0602) 240000

Nottinghamshire **n** County Council
Planning & Economic Development